CIVICS, LAW, AND JUSTICE—HOW WE BECAME U.S.

CIVICS, LAW, AND JUSTICE—HOW WE BECAME U.S.

Insights from a Trial Judge

J. LAYNE SMITH

Contact the publisher at askjudgesmith@gmail.com or askjudgesmith.com.

ISBN 978-1-7345669-0-1 (printed book)

ISBN 978-1-7345669-1-8 (e-book)

ISBN 978-1-7345669-2-5 (audiobook)

Disclaimer

This book is intended for educational and informational purposes only. The author is not rendering legal advice and no attorney-client relationship exists between the author and the reader.

I dedicate this book to Abraham Lincoln and my wife,
but mostly to my wife!

TABLE OF CONTENTS

About the Author 221

Dedication v

Foreword xi

PART I FUNDAMENTALS OF THE U.S. CONSTITUTION AND BILL OF RIGHTS

Chapter 1 Talking Taxes and the French and Indian War 3

Chapter 2 Give Me Whataburger or Give Me Death 5

Chapter 3 Out with the Old and In with the New 9

Chapter 4 A Sprint Through the Bill of Rights 13

Chapter 5 The Goldilocks Government 17

Chapter 6 Henry, the Ignoble Noble 21

Chapter 7 Civics and Sausage 25

Chapter 8 The Magnificent Seven 29

Chapter 9 Checks, Balances, and Flag Burning 33

Chapter 10 Doubting Thomas and the Pledge of Allegiance 37

Chapter 11 What's Your Knowledge of the Electoral College? 41

Chapter 12 Thanksgiving from a Most Unlikely Source 45

Chapter 13 Republic or Democracy—Sue Wants to Know 49

PART II INSIGHTS FROM A TRIAL JUDGE

Chapter 14 Jigsaw Justice—Piecing Trials Together 55

Chapter 15 The Little Engine that Could 59

Chapter 16 Courts See the Good, the Bad, and the Ugly 63
Chapter 17 Expectations and Sentencing 65
Chapter 18 Two-Sided Pancakes 69
Chapter 19 Appointed and Elected Judges 73
Chapter 20 When Duty Conflicts with Faith 77
Chapter 21 The Sound of Silence 81
Chapter 22 Like Peas and Carrots 85
Chapter 23 Merry Christmas from the Leon County Jail 89

PART III BEING THE JURY

Chapter 24 Fair and Impartial Juries 95
Chapter 25 My Patriotic, Flag-Waving, Jury Service Speech 99
Chapter 26 What Juries Don't Hear at Trial 103
Chapter 27 Sunshine and Sequestration 107
Chapter 28 Anniversaries and Affirmations 111

PART IV ANSWERS TO BASIC LEGAL QUESTIONS

Chapter 29 Lincoln's Logic 117
Chapter 30 She Slashed a Hole in All Four Tires 121
Chapter 31 Caesar and Gollum Explain Latin 125
Chapter 32 Marshal Dillon to the Rescue 129
Chapter 33 Jobs, Welfare, or Crime 133
Chapter 34 Juggling Chainsaws 137
Chapter 35 Stand and Be Counted 141
Chapter 36 Ostriches and Blabbermouths Lose Cases 145
Chapter 37 To Plea or Not to Plea 149
Chapter 38 Avoiding the Shark's House 153
Chapter 39 Newtonian Physics and Violations of Probation 157
Chapter 40 Boxing, Wrestling, and Cases in Controversy 161

Chapter 41 I Say, You Say, Earl Say, Hearsay 165
Chapter 42 The ABCs of Attorney Fees 169
Chapter 43 Professor Plum Gets a Clue 173
Chapter 44 Inquests of the Dead 177
Chapter 45 Signs and Interventions 181
Chapter 46 Notice and an Opportunity to be Heard 183

PART V BEING A LAWYER

Chapter 47 The Benefit of Experience 189
Chapter 48 Becoming Lawyers 193
Chapter 49 Letter to a Law School Graduate 195
Chapter 50 Murder, Cannibalism, and Government Conspiracy 199
Chapter 51 The Lawyers Know Too Much 203

PART VI GOING FORWARD

Chapter 52 Dad Was Special and Plan While You Can 209
Chapter 53 Rhett Butler and E Pluribus Unum 213
Chapter 54 Time Travel and Keeping It Real 215
Acknowledgements 219

FOREWORD

One morning over breakfast with a friend, I told her I'd like to write a legal column for our local newspaper. By the time we finished our meal, it had been arranged, and my newspaper column provided source material for this book.

My goal is to answer common questions about civics, law, and justice and to make our federal and state courts less mysterious and more accessible. We'll focus on the big picture.

Please understand that as a judge, I must remain neutral and removed from politics, and cannot express opinions about what our public policy should be.

I hope you enjoy my book and I am hard at work on the next one.

Respectfully,

J. Layne Smith
Leon County Judge
Florida's Second Judicial Circuit

PART I

FUNDAMENTALS OF THE U.S. CONSTITUTION AND BILL OF RIGHTS

CHAPTER 1

TALKING TAXES AND THE FRENCH AND INDIAN WAR

Our discussion of government and American justice begins with the French and Indian War. This conflict began in 1756 when local Indian tribes allied with the French and fought against the British expansion.

In response, American colonists formed their first continental army to fight in the war; however, the army was inadequately financed, poorly trained and largely ineffective. The British Army joined the fray, but for years fared no better. Eventually, Great Britain won the war by building up and maintaining a large-standing North American army and then taking the fight to the French and their Native American allies throughout the continent.

The French and Indian War lasted seven years, and the cost of winning the war and maintaining the peace afterward created a huge debt for the British Empire. In response, Parliament imposed heavy regressive taxes on American colonists, while simultaneously denying them the right to vote in Great Britain's Parliamentary elections.

Our Founding Fathers bristled at this situation.

They were required to obey British laws and be loyal subjects, but their rights were dramatically restricted. They were prohibited from gathering, their speech was censored, and they couldn't print what they wanted to say in their newspapers or other publications.

British military and law enforcement officers searched colonists and their properties without cause, and American colonists were arrested, jailed, and held indefinitely without being told why. They had no right to counsel, no right to a trial by a jury of their peers, and these trials were not open to the public. Criminal defendants were forced to testify; otherwise, their silence was used to incriminate them.

The combination of taxation without representation and these legal injustices sowed the seeds of the American Revolution. If the French and Indian War had never happened, our legal system would be dramatically different. And I'd probably have to wear one of those funny white, powdered wigs in the courtroom.

CHAPTER 2

GIVE ME WHATABURGER OR GIVE ME DEATH

Imagine, if you will, being the first settler of an American colony. Having crossed the Atlantic Ocean in a boat roughly the size of the S. S. Minnow, you disembark into the wilderness. There is nothing else. No Publix, no WHATABURGER, no hospital, no infrastructure.

The first American colonists had a lot in common with the survivalists on the series "Naked and Afraid." If not for their fierce independence and self-reliance, we might still be part of the British Empire.

As "western civilization" took root, each colony established a legislature and enjoyed limited self-rule. The colonists chafed when Great Britain imposed taxes and restricted their freedoms. War followed, and in the Declaration of Independence, each colony withdrew its allegiance to Great Britain and declared itself to be a "free and independent state."

Congress and the 13 states established our first national government by ratifying the Articles of Confederation. In it, each state retained its "sovereignty, freedom, and independence." Flashpoints quickly arose:

1) The federal government was too weak and underfunded to properly function.

2) Citizens from one state couldn't get fair trials in the courts of other states.

3) Shays' Rebellion exposed the nation's vulnerability to armed mobs.

Ultimately, the Articles of Confederation were too flawed to fix. Our Founders' dilemma was how to create a stronger national government without empowering a tyrant. Their solution was to propose a Constitution that would:

1) Provide government with specific but limited powers.

2) Divide the powers of government among three independent and co-equal branches.

3) Provide checks and balances to prevent any one branch or person from amassing too much power.

All other governmental powers were to remain vested in the states.

The devil, of course, was in the details. Let's consider three examples. The proposed Constitution would empower the federal government to:

1) Lay and collect taxes and provide for the common defense and general welfare of the United States.

2) Regulate commerce with foreign nations, among the several states, and with the Native Americans tribes.

3) Make all laws "necessary and proper" for executing its Constitutional powers.

The Federalists wanted a stronger and more active national government. They argued that these powers were necessary and sufficiently limited. They emphasized the desperate need for change.

The Anti-Federalists preferred a weaker and more passive national government. They argued that these powers were too broad and warned that each one would be twisted to extend federal reach. As such, the states' sovereignty and the people's rights would be at risk.

Next, we will discuss the arguments for and against ratifying the Constitution and the Bill of Rights (the first 10 Amendments).

CHAPTER 3

OUT WITH THE OLD AND IN WITH THE NEW

The Revolutionary War began in 1775 and ended in 1783. It spanned over 8 years (101 months). During that time, many American soldiers received little to no pay for their military service. After the war ended, Congress couldn't satisfy the nation's war debts, including soldiers' back pay. Chronically short of funds, the federal government caused runaway inflation by over-circulating worthless paper money. Farmers were hit hard, and many lost their farms to foreclosures.

In 1786-1787, armed mobs looted stores in rural Massachusetts. In January 1787, Daniel Shays lead 1,500 rebels in an attack on the armory in Springfield, Massachusetts. These rebels intended to seize its weaponry and overthrow the state's government. The federal government was unable to muster any military response. Instead, a privately funded state militia squashed Shays' Rebellion.

In May 1787, the Constitutional Convention met in Philadelphia. There, our Founders proposed scrapping the Articles of Confederation and replacing it with a new federal government under a Constitution.

Having been ratified by Congress and the legislatures of all 13 states, the Articles of Confederation could only be dissolved by unanimous consent. Lacking unanimity, the Constitutional Convention baldly asserted that the Constitution would take effect if ratified by Congress and at least nine states. Even so, everyone feared that anything short of a ratification by all 13 states would result in anarchy.

The Federalists, led by George Washington and Alexander Hamilton, wanted to empower the federal government to raise taxes, satisfy the war debts, and regulate commerce. They supported ratifying the Constitution.

The Anti-Federalists, led by Thomas Jefferson and James Monroe, didn't want to strengthen the federal government. They believed doing so would be at the expense of the people and the sovereign states. Anti-Federalists opposed ratifying the Constitution.

The Federalists believed that the proposed Constitution would provide a strong and flexible government that would adequately protect the people's rights. They argued against adding amendments because the new federal government's powers would already be limited to those specifically delegated to it by the people.

The Anti-Federalists couldn't raise enough support to save

the Articles of Confederation. Likewise, they couldn't sway enough state legislatures to scuttle ratification of the Constitution by at least nine states. However, they could generate enough opposition to prevent its unanimous ratification by all 13 states. This clout turned out to be just enough leverage to negotiate a compromise.

Anti-Federalists agreed to ratify the Constitution if it included 10 amendments, which became known as the Bill of Rights. The purpose of these amendments was to protect the people's individual rights against tyranny and to prevent the national government from usurping the states' sovereignty.

Even with this compromise, ratification by every state was no slam-dunk. On May 29, 1790, by a vote of 34-32, Rhode Island was the 13th and final state to ratify the Constitution, as amended. Anyone who listens to CNN or FOX news can still hear the echoes of Federalists' and Anti-Federalists' arguments playing out.

CHAPTER 4

A SPRINT THROUGH THE BILL OF RIGHTS

Before the Revolutionary War, British troops occupied Boston and imposed martial law. Throughout the colonies, colonists were not allowed to gather, speak freely or publish anything critical of British rule. British officials searched people and private property whenever they felt like it, and forcibly housed their troops in American homes without permission or compensation. Following hunches and gossip, they arrested and jailed people without cause.

With this background, our Founders had good reasons to fear tyrants and centralized authority. Their fears led to the creation of the Bill of Rights. That said, let's review what the Bill of Rights does for us.

First Amendment

Congress can't establish a state religion, tell you how to worship, keep you from expressing your thoughts, or censor or shut down the media. It can't prevent people from gathering peacefully. And people can petition the government for relief, which means they can make complaints, sue the government, and lobby it for change.

Second Amendment (exactly as written)

A well-regulated militia, being necessary to the security of a free state, the right of the people to keep and bear arms, shall not be infringed.

Third Amendment

The government can't force people to house soldiers in their homes during times of peace. During wartime, it can only do so as prescribed by law.

Fourth Amendment

The Fourth Amendment protects people's privacy. Government can't conduct unreasonable searches and seizures of persons or private property, but can conduct searches and seizures that have been authorized by search warrants.

Judges can issue search warrants on findings of probable cause supported by sworn testimony. Search warrants must describe with particularity the places to be searched and the things to be seized.

Fifth Amendment

Only a grand jury can bring certain criminal charges against defendants. Anyone found not guilty of an offense can't be retried for the same offense, and people's property can't be taken from them unless they're fairly compensated.

Criminal defendants cannot be forced to testify about the charges against them, and they will not face any repercussions for remaining silent. A person's life, liberty, or property can't be taken from them without "due process of law."

Sixth Amendment

Criminal defendants must be informed of the specific charges against them so they can defend themselves. They have the right to speedy and public trials by impartial juries. They have the right to counsel, to confront opposing witnesses, and to present defenses.

Seventh Amendment

A person has the right to a jury trial in a civil lawsuit if certain thresholds are met.

Eighth Amendment (exactly as written)

Excessive bail shall not be required, nor excessive fines imposed, nor cruel and unusual punishment inflicted.

Ninth Amendment

People have more rights than those listed in the Constitution.

Tenth Amendment

The states keep all powers the Constitution does not expressly delegate to the federal government nor deny to the states.

CHAPTER 5
THE GOLDILOCKS GOVERNMENT

American colonists were women and men of action. They tended to be independent thinkers and pioneers. They asked King George III to repeal several unpopular laws and to allow them limited self-rule and equality. He flatly refused. Instead, the crown asserted tighter control, which sparked open rebellion.

You have heard the saying that absolute power corrupts absolutely. As a people, we have never trusted highly centralized authority. We have always equated kings and "strong men" with tyrants. Nobody likes a micro-managing bully!

Afraid of replacing one tyrant with another, the national government we formed under The Articles of Confederation was too weak and too decentralized to work. Our Founders' dilemma was how to strengthen a new federal government without empowering another tyrant.

Government under a king was too tyrannical. Government under The Articles of Confederation was too weak and ineffective. Like Goldilocks, our Founders sought a government that would be "just right." Their solution was The United States Constitution and The Bill of Rights.

Think of our federal government as a three-legged stool. You cannot safely sit on a three-legged stool unless each leg is the same length, strong enough, and equidistant from one another. Perfect balance is required.

The United States Constitution limits government by dividing its powers among three separate, independent, and co-equal branches (the legislative, the executive, and the judicial). Ever wary of the power-hungry, The United States Constitution also imposes a series of checks and balances to prevent any one person or branch from accumulating too much power.

As a failsafe, our Founders added The Bill of Rights to protect the people from government abuses and tyrants. As a result, America is the land of hope and opportunity, and the envy of the world.

Our Founders understood human nature and human fallibility, too. They created an independent and self-regulating judiciary to remove politics from the administration of justice. Judges must follow the rule of law without regard to who the parties are, or what the popular sentiment of the day is.

An independent and self-regulated legal profession protects judges, lawyers, and you from undue government domination by the executive and legislative branches.

Lawyers play a unique role in government because only they can serve the public as judges. No other profession is solely responsible for a branch of government.

CHAPTER 6

HENRY, THE IGNOBLE NOBLE

Although he has been dead for more than 471 years, King Henry VIII continues to fascinate us, and nobody likes him better than the entertainment industry. Henry's life and reign are featured on the BBC's series "Wolf Hall," Showtime's series "The Tudors," and the Academy Award-winning movie "A Man for All Seasons."

Most people remember Henry for having six wives. He was so desperate to father a male heir that he beheaded two wives and annulled marriages to two others. Ironically, it was Henry's infertility that prevented him from having more children.

Aside from his family issues, Henry was a ruthless tyrant and a self-centered jerk. He placed himself above the law and domineered parliament and his subjects. Henry imprisoned, tortured, and killed his subjects with impunity and without due process of law. He also got his way by bribery, patronage, and coercion.

Henry lived the high life and financed his reign by confiscating the assets of the Catholic Church and the private property of his subjects.

By "nationalizing" the assets of others without paying them any compensation, Henry served as a role-model for future communists.

Henry established a state religion, censored free speech, restricted a free press, and prevented people from peaceably assembling or petitioning his government for redress of their grievances (think the First Amendment).

His henchmen regularly searched people and seized private property without lawful justification (think the Fourth Amendment).

In addition to taking others' property without due process of law or compensation, Henry compelled defendants to testify against themselves, and he used their silence to incriminate them (think the Fifth Amendment).

He eliminated some foes without making any formal charges against them. Others were denied the right to counsel and weren't allowed to present defenses. They couldn't confront adverse witnesses, compel favorable evidence, or have their cases decided by fair and impartial juries (think the Sixth Amendment).

Finally, during Henry's reign people were caged, racked, starved, or otherwise tortured. Some were executed by being burned at the stake, boiled alive, or disemboweled. Cruelness was regularly practiced to discourage resistance (think the Eighth Amendment).

Our Founders knew English history and they were aware of Henry VIII's chronic abuses of power. To protect us from like-minded tyrants, the federal government they formed divides its powers among three equal branches and employs a system of checks and balances. Henry VIII's infamy was a catalyst for the First, Fourth, Fifth, Sixth, and Eighth Amendments to the U. S. Constitution.

Henry VIII was an ignoble noble. Perhaps had he been less tyrannical and better behaved, our Bill of Rights would read much differently.

CHAPTER 7

CIVICS AND SAUSAGE

On Saturday mornings I enjoy having breakfast with my parents. Last week, Mom asked me to explain state government. After my first cup of coffee had kicked in, this is what I told her.

There are three independent and equal branches of state government —the legislature, the executive, and the judicial. Florida is governed by a constitution that lists the powers and responsibilities of each branch.

The Florida Legislature passes laws and the state's budget each year. This is the branch that develops the state's public policy, which is enacted when the governor (in the executive branch) signs bills into law. The executive branch also enforces the law through the governor and three independently elected Cabinet officers: the attorney general; the commissioner of agriculture; and the chief financial officer.

The third branch is the judicial branch or court system.

People appreciate a judiciary that consistently and efficiently applies the rule of law. It's like having a good umpire that calls a fair and consistent strike zone each game—you know what you are going to get, no matter which team is at bat.

As part of the judicial branch, judges interpret and apply the law, and resolve criminal, civil, and family law cases. The judiciary's priorities include ensuring due process, equal justice, and fair, impartial, and transparent proceedings. Hearings and trials are open to the public, and a record is made of every criminal proceeding. Cameras and television coverage are common in courtrooms. Courts cannot function without the people's trust.

County and circuit courts are courts of original jurisdiction, which means each case is tried before a single judge, one at a time. The 67 county courts handle the largest volume of cases, largely consisting of misdemeanor charges, small claims up to $8,000, and civil cases involving between $8,000 and $30,000. Circuit courts handle the more complex cases—felony charges, civil cases involving more than $30,000, juvenile cases, probate cases, family law cases, and injunctions. Circuit judges also hear appeals of county court decisions.

The five District Courts of Appeal hear appeals of circuit court decisions and final state agency actions. The Florida Supreme Court hears appeals from the District Courts of Appeal and reviews all final orders imposing the death sentence and bond validations. The Supreme Court approves the standard jury instructions and rules of procedure used by trial courts. It also disciplines wayward attorneys and judges.

We inherited many legal precedents from English courts, collectively known as the "common law," and Florida courts routinely issue written orders and opinions known as "case law." Imagine, if you will, that Florida law is shaped like a pyramid. The state's constitution occupies the top tier. If there is any conflict between the constitution and a statute, a case law, or an executive order, the constitution wins. Florida statutes occupy the middle tier. If there is any conflict between a statute and case law or an executive order, the statute wins. Case law, executive orders, and state agency rules occupy the bottom tier of the pyramid.

The civics lesson ended when the food arrived.

CHAPTER 8

THE MAGNIFICENT SEVEN

Q. Judge Smith, would you explain the importance of the Sixth Amendment? Thank you, Hal

A. Hal, the Sixth Amendment provides seven distinct and fundamental rights for criminal defendants. These rights are so important I call them "the magnificent seven." Let's take them in order.

<u>1. The Right to a Speedy Trial</u>

American colonists lacked the right to a speedy trial, and many were arrested, confined, and left to languish. The Sixth Amendment prevents this fate.

<u>2. The Right to a Public Trial</u>

The British excluded the public from observing a criminal trial if the Crown deemed the case to be sensitive. Private trials undermine the public's confidence in due process and the rule of law. The right to a public trial protects defendants from malevolent prosecutors, corrupt or malleable judges, lying witnesses, and jurors susceptible to taking bribes. Transparency and accountability promote the people's confidence in justice and the judiciary.

3. The Right to an Impartial Jury

The Sixth Amendment ensures a jury pool will represent a fair cross-section of the defendant's local community. Jurors answer questions under oath and provide information about themselves. They swear or affirm they will be fair, impartial, and follow courts' instructions on the law.

4. The Right to be Informed of Pending Charges

The Crown abused its police power by arresting and jailing people without charging them with any crimes. The Sixth Amendment requires the government to inform defendants of the specific charges against them so they can defend themselves.

5. The Right to Confront Adverse Witnesses

The government bears the burden of proving beyond a reasonable doubt that the charged crime was committed, and the defendant is the person who committed the crime. Defendants can confront and cross-examine the witnesses that testifies against them.

6. The Right to Compel Favorable Evidence

Trials aren't one-way streets traveled solely by prosecutors. Defendants also can call witnesses, put on evidence, and make an appellate record. The Sixth Amendment empowers defendants to use courts' compulsory subpoena power to compel favorable testimony and evidence at trial.

7. The Right to Legal Counsel

Defendants have the right to counsel when the government initiates adversarial criminal proceedings against them. If a defendant is denied counsel at any critical stage of the case, a subsequent conviction would be unconstitutional and reversed.

Our Founders feared tyrants, distrusted centralized authority, and worried about government oppression. By design, these seven Sixth Amendment rights work in tandem to protect our lives and liberty from abuses by would-be tyrants. Thus, we are spared unjust confinements.

CHAPTER 9

CHECKS, BALANCES, AND FLAG BURNING

Our Founding Fathers loathed tyrants, so they worked hard to create a better functioning national government that protected the rights of the people and the sovereignty of the states. Their solution was to separate the powers of government among the legislative, executive, and judicial branches so no person or branch would accumulate too much power.

Additionally, they provided a system of checks and balances each branch can employ to prevent another branch from overreaching. Let's identify some of those checks and balances.

Executive Branch Checks and Balances

- The President can veto laws passed by Congress.
- The President nominates federal judges for confirmation by the Senate.

Legislative Branch Checks and Balances

- By a two-thirds supermajority vote, Congress can override presidential vetoes.
- The House can impeach, and the Senate can remove the President from office.
- The Senate can reject the President's judicial nominees.
- The House can impeach, and the Senate can remove federal judges from office.
- Congress and the states' legislatures can amend the Constitution.

Judicial Branch Checks and Balances

- Federal judges can invalidate unconstitutional laws.

Flag Burning

Let's use an example from history to better illustrate how the checks and balances work. Freedom of speech from government interference covers more than the spoken and written word. It also extends to conduct intended to convey a specific message that viewers are likely to see and understand, even if they vehemently disagree!

For example, the State of Texas enacted a criminal law that prohibited the desecration of an American flag. Afterward, a self-described communist poured kerosene on an American flag and burned it. Texas prosecuted, convicted, and sentenced him to a year in prison.

The U.S. Supreme Court reversed the defendant's conviction on appeal because the Texas law violated his First Amendment right to free speech.

In response, Congress passed the "Flag Protection Act." The President could have vetoed the law, but he didn't. If he had, Congress could have overridden his veto by a supermajority vote. The U.S. Supreme Court then struck down the "Flag Protection Act" as unconstitutional because it too violated the First Amendment right to free speech.

Both Supreme Court decisions to strike down the federal law and the Texas law prohibiting flag burning were unpopular. In response, Congress proposed a Constitutional amendment that, if ratified, would have allowed it to criminalize the physical desecration of the nation's flag. However, the proposed constitutional amendment was never voted out of Congress. Had it been, at least 38 state legislatures would have had to ratify the new amendment to make it the law.

In this real-life example, the judiciary checked overreaches by the legislative branch, and Congress still tried to get its way by amending the Constitution. That's how checks and balances work.

CHAPTER 10

DOUBTING THOMAS AND THE PLEDGE OF ALLEGIANCE

Q. Judge Smith, after watching the U.S. Supreme Court confirmation hearings, I'm curious why each state, regardless of its population, has two U.S. Senators? In a democracy, does that not give smaller states an unfair advantage? Thank you, Thomas.

A. Thomas, your questions are hot topics of discussion since the recent confirmation hearings, and you are not the only person to express doubts. Let's look to civics and history for context.

Do you remember the line in the Pledge of Allegiance that says, "…and to the Republic for which it stands…?" Contrary to popular belief, the United States of America is a republic, not a democracy. Through democratic elections, we choose representatives and senators to decide political issues and set policy for us.

Before the constitution was ratified, each state was sovereign and jealously guarded its independence. Understandably, less-populated states feared their sovereignty would be overtaken by the more-populated states if representation in Congress was based solely on population. Likewise, more-populated states feared their sovereignty would be unfairly diluted unless representation in Congress was based solely on population. The solution was a bicameral Congress that addressed both concerns.

In the House of Representatives, seats are apportioned based on population, with each state being guaranteed at least one seat. In the Senate, each state gets two senators regardless of its population. This combination is fair because it balances out disparities, and legislation must pass in both houses.

As an example, let's compare the most-populated state to the least-populated state. California and Wyoming each have two Senators and possess equal strength in the Senate. In contrast, California has 53 seats and Wyoming has one seat in the House of Representatives.

To provide some perspective, California has more seats in the House of Representatives than these 21 states combined:

Alaska, Arkansas, Delaware, Hawaii, Idaho, Iowa, Kansas, Maine, Mississippi, Montana, Nebraska, New Hampshire, New Mexico, North Dakota, Oklahoma, Rhode Island, South Dakota, Utah, Vermont, West Virginia, and Wyoming.

Because the Senate confirms judges, every state has an equal say. If instead, the House of Representatives had the authority to confirm judges, the most-populated states would decide the federal judgeships for everyone else. Rest assured that Wyoming doesn't want California dictating who its federal district judges are going to be. Thomas, I hope this helps.

CHAPTER 11

WHAT'S YOUR KNOWLEDGE OF THE ELECTORAL COLLEGE?

Q. Judge Smith, please explain how a presidential candidate can win the popular vote and lose the election? — Kendra

A. Kendra, it's because presidents aren't elected in national elections. Instead, they are elected based on the combined results of 51 separate elections conducted by the fifty states and the District of Columbia.

Historically, the 13 original colonies declared themselves to be independent and sovereign states. Our Founders thought themselves to be citizens of their home states, and they considered their national citizenship to be of secondary importance. The people who lived in a particular state tended to trust local people, local government, and local solutions over "strangers governing from afar."

Our nation is an oddity because it's comprised of 50 sovereign states and a federal government. Most powers are reserved to the states, and the federal government's powers are limited to those ceded to it by the people.

When our Founders wrote the Constitution, they debated how the chief executive officer of the federal government should be chosen. One faction wanted the chief executive to be elected by a majority vote of Congress. Another faction wanted the president to be elected directly by the combined national vote of the people. Neither faction prevailed.

Each state was used to electing its governor—the chief executive officer of the state—in state-wide races where the winner took all. It didn't matter if a governor won his race by one vote or 100,000 votes. The less populated states feared that the direct election of presidents by the combined national vote would dilute the choice of its people. Based on their preference for a winner-takes-all result, the Founders decided that presidents shall be elected based on each state's vote.

Each state is allocated an electoral vote for each member of its Congressional delegation, and the District of Columbia is allocated three electoral votes. Each presidential candidate selects a slate of electors to cast the state's electoral votes for him or her if he or she wins that state's vote. So, instead of voting for a particular presidential candidate, you are really voting for that candidate's slate of electors.

The U.S. Constitution treats presidential elections as the separate vote of the 50 sovereign states. Forty-eight states award all of their electoral votes to the candidate who receives the most statewide votes. Maine and Nebraska differ by awarding one electoral vote to the candidate who wins each congressional district.

Let's finish with an example involving two states and two candidates. John Jones wins the general election for president in California by a mere 5,000 votes. As the state's top vote-getter, he wins all 55 of California's electoral votes. Jenny Smith wins the general election for president in Wyoming by a comfortable 106,000 votes. As the state's top vote-getter, she wins all three of Wyoming's electoral votes. Combining these results, John Jones wins 52 more electoral votes than Jenny Smith, even though she outpolled him by 101,000 votes. This example shows how a presidential candidate can win the popular vote and still lose the election.

A presidential candidate must win at least 270 out of 538 electoral votes to be elected president. I hope that helps.

CHAPTER 12

THANKSGIVING FROM A MOST UNLIKELY SOURCE

It's ironic that our annual celebration of the Thanksgiving holiday was started by a man of sorrows. Born poor, lacking formal education, and suffering through the death of his mother at a tender age, no one expected much from Abraham Lincoln. He suffered from depression his entire life.

His appearance didn't help either. Lincoln was unusually tall, thin, and gawky. In addition to being "just plain ugly," his voice was high-pitched and often sounded whiny.

Lincoln failed at business, struggled to pay bills, and suffered the death of his one true love; he also had a mental breakdown and a long convalescence. Lincoln's wife battled her own mental health issues, and her instability weighed him down, too. Yet Lincoln rose above these obstacles to become one of the preeminent trial lawyers of his day.

Lincoln was not a political superstar. Prior to 1860, he lost eight political elections and was never elected to a statewide office. When he was elected president, 11 southern states rebelled, and the Civil War followed. Everyone grossly underestimated the man and his strength of character, and probably for good reason.

The Civil War raged from April 12, 1861, through May 9, 1865. The Union had superior resources and the moral high ground, but Lincoln lacked an effective military leader to take the fight to the South. That changed on March 9, 1864, when he appointed Ulysses Grant as commander of the Union Army.

Consider this sobering statistic: Many more Americans died or were wounded fighting the Civil War than in any other American conflict. Lincoln tracked the cost in blood, and wrote many letters of condolence to grieving parents, wives, and children.

I've included two photographs of President Lincoln to demonstrate the impact that the stress of the war had on him. The first picture was taken in 1861, after he had been elected president. The second picture was taken in 1865, after he had won a bitterly contested re-election campaign and shortly before he was assassinated. During the intervening four years, Lincoln suffered through the deaths of more than 600,000 soldiers and his beloved 11-year-old son, Willie. He literally aged decades in the span of 48 months.

Lesser men would have soured on life and become pessimists. Instead, he purposefully chose to be an optimist, despite all the pain and uncertainties he faced. On October 3, 1863, Lincoln issued a presidential proclamation that established our nation's annual celebration of the Thanksgiving holiday.

If Lincoln could be thankful in the midst of his troubles, so can we. If he could hold everything together for the equality of mankind and for good of our nation, so can we. Indeed, we owe him that. Each Thanksgiving, let's count our many blessings, pray for one another, and heed President Lincoln's warning that "a house divided against itself cannot stand" (Mark 3:25).

CHAPTER 13

REPUBLIC OR DEMOCRACY—SUE WANTS TO KNOW

Q. Judge Smith, I'm in middle school and want to be a lawyer when I grow up. Which do you think is better, a republic or a democracy? — Sue

A. Sue, you have the perfect name for a lawyer! All kidding aside, I'm delighted that you want to be one. Now, let's discuss republics and democracies.

The most noteworthy ancient republic was Rome before it became an empire. In fact, the word *republic* is derived from the Latin phrase *res publica,* which means "the laws." The Roman republic was governed by a senate, who established its laws. Roman senators were wealthy male aristocrats. They weren't elected by the people.

Both our federal and state governments are republics. When I became a lawyer, and later when I became a county judge,

I swore an oath to support, protect, and defend the constitutions and governments of the United States and of the State of Florida. I have always lived faithfully by those oaths. As a future lawyer, one day you'll take a similar oath when you become a member of a state's bar.

In our Republic, the people don't directly vote on every political issue. Instead, through the democratic process, we elect senators and representatives who decide political issues and establish public policy on our behalf. While the majority tends to get its way, "the laws" protect us from the "tyranny of the mob" that might otherwise follow. Both the constitution and our courts' faithful application of the rule of law prevent the majority from running roughshod over minorities and people with unpopular views.

The most noteworthy ancient democracies were the Greek city-states. The word democracy is derived from the Greek words *demos* and *kratein*, which mean "the people to rule." In a democracy, political issues are decided by a majority vote of the people. Democracies don't protect minorities and people with unpopular views. Also, while democracies might be practical in small city-states, democracies are too unwieldy to function in large nations. Imagine how impractical and expensive it would be to hold national elections on every political issue that confronts us, much less the potential for recounts!

In 1787, the Constitutional Convention met in private. When it adjourned, the public did not know which form of government the delegates were recommending. When asked by a curious Philadelphian if it was to be a republic or a monarchy, Benjamin Franklin responded, "A republic, if you can keep it." Two centuries later, President Reagan rightly described the American people and our government as "the last best hope of man on earth."

My direct answer to your question is less important than what you think. Given my explanation of the two, which form of government do you think is best?

Sue, behave, study hard, and respect your elders. I invite you to schedule a day during your summer vacation to visit the courthouse and shadow a judge. Stay curious and think for yourself!

PART II

INSIGHTS FROM A TRIAL JUDGE

CHAPTER 14

JIGSAW JUSTICE—PIECING TRIALS TOGETHER

Every trial involves elements, a burden of proof, and a standard of proof. Today, I'm going to use a jigsaw puzzle to explain these concepts.

Have you ever spent a rainy-day piecing together a puzzle? Thank goodness for the picture on the box cover. Without that image, you wouldn't know what you're trying to assemble and all you'd have is a jumble of pieces.

In many ways, trials are like jigsaw puzzles.

Elements

Civil causes of action and criminal charges are comprised of "elements" that plaintiffs and prosecutors must prove to win their cases. By analogy, the elements of a case are the puzzle pieces.

The Burden of Proof

The burden of proof governs who must assemble the puzzle. Plaintiffs and prosecutors must present evidence in support of their claims. They bear the burden of proof. In a civil case, the plaintiff must prove the defendant's liability and the amount of damages due. In a criminal case, the prosecutor must prove the crime was committed, and the defendant did it.

Standards of Proof

Standards of proof impose quality controls that govern how juries decide cases.

Usually, plaintiffs must prove their claims by the "greater weight of the evidence." This means a plaintiff must persuade the jury that his or her claim is probably true.

Some claims require plaintiffs to prove their claims by "clear and convincing evidence." This means a plaintiff must persuade the jury to firmly believe that his or her claim is true.

In criminal cases, prosecutors must prove their cases "beyond a reasonable doubt." This means the prosecutor must persuade the jury of the defendant's guilt, by eliminating all reasonable doubt that he committed the crime.

Now, let's tie everything together with two examples.

Breach of Contract

A bank sues a borrower for defaulting on a loan. To win its claim for breach of contract, the bank must prove three elements by the greater weight of the evidence:

1) The parties had a contract;

2) The defendant breached the contract; and

3) The plaintiff has sustained damages due to the breach.

<u>Criminal Battery</u>

A man punches his neighbor. The state charges him with criminal battery. To win at trial, the state must prove one of the following two elements beyond a reasonable doubt:

1) The defendant intentionally touched or struck the neighbor against his will; or

2) The defendant intentionally caused bodily harm to the neighbor.

I hope you find this information to be helpful, and not too puzzling.

CHAPTER 15

THE LITTLE ENGINE THAT COULD

When I was a small child, my mother read me stories with morals, and one of my favorites was "The Little Engine That Could." In the story, a determined little engine pulls a heavy-laden train up a mountain to deliver food and toys to children. The lesson extols the values of optimism and work ethic. As it turns out, "The Little Engine That Could" is the perfect metaphor for your county court.

Like the hero of the story, your county court carries a heavy caseload. During fiscal year 2017-2018, 72 percent of the new cases opened in Leon County were filed in the county court. As a result, 32,778 cases were divided among the five county judges.

County judges' criminal dockets cover misdemeanor cases, and their civil dockets cover:

1) Landlord-tenant evictions;

2) Garnishments;

3) Small claims involving $8,000 or less;

4) Civil claims between $8,000 and $30,000; and

5) Traffic infractions involving serious bodily injuries.

Most civil cases involve at least one person who represents himself without counsel. Because non-lawyers lack legal training and experience, judges must devote additional time to assure due process of law and decisions on the merits.

County judges preside over specialty courts, which include:

1) Veterans Treatment Court;

2) Drug and Alcohol Rehabilitation Court;

3) Mental Health Court; and

4) Drivers' License Clinics.

Specialty courts address far reaching societal problems and require a significant investment of judicial time, which we alone provide.

Every day, county judges also cover circuit court work, including:

1) Felony first appearances and extraditions;

2) Felony search and arrest warrants;

3) Jury qualification;

4) Baker Act hearings to compel psychiatric treatment;

5) Marchman Act hearings to compel substance abuse treatment;

6) Risk Protection Order hearings to take firearms, ammunition, and weapons from people threatening suicide or murder;

7) Family court adoptions, uncontested divorces, and name changes; and

8) Injunction hearings to protect victims of domestic, repeat, sexual, or dating violence, or stalking.

Our handling of these circuit court duties enables the circuit judges to focus on their most serious, demanding and complicated cases, including ones with statewide implications.

Both Florida's and Leon County's populations are growing! As they increase, so too will the workloads that are assigned to the county judges.

Like "The Little Engine That Could," your county court "thinks it can" and remains optimistic and hard at work.

CHAPTER 16

COURTS SEE THE GOOD, THE BAD, AND THE UGLY

My title doesn't concern the punchline of a joke promoting Seminole athletics or a review of the Clint Eastwood western with the awesome theme song. Instead, my focus is on the human condition and hope.

As your county judge, I'm responsible for independently reviewing the factual basis for arrests, searches, and seizures. Frankly, you wouldn't believe what I read and hear daily—ranging from the comic to the tragic. Truth is indeed stranger than fiction, and television is filled with crime shows because the material writes itself. Regardless, everyone deserves due process of law and an equal application of the rule of law.

Now, let's discuss the good, the bad, and the ugly. The good function as the glue that holds society together by being fair, honest, kind, decent, and reliable. They care for the welfare of others. The bad commit intentional wrongs, have lapses of judgment, and are less reliable. "Bad" doesn't have to be a permanent condition, and our nation is the land of opportunity and second chances. The ugly commit premeditated murders, torture, rapes, and other horrific crimes without regard to the misery and harm they cause.

Now for the call to action. The good are needed now more than ever. Hurricane Michael devastated a 70-mile swath of the Florida Panhandle. Its victims include friends, neighbors, kids, older folks, and the poor. These vulnerable souls are in desperate need of immediate help, and it will require the kindness of strangers to help them survive and recover.

Happily, many first responders, people, charities, and organizations are working hard to make a meaningful difference. Let's thank them, provide encouragement, and help the helpers.

As generous and compassionate people, the good also need to be the helpers. For example, The William H. Stafford American Inn of Court has more than 100 members from the local legal community. Each member has agreed to provide at least 10 hours of community service work for hurricane victims, including their pets. This alone will result in more than 1,000 hours of help for those in need!

I close with this observation. People are suffering and in need of hope. Let's respond with kindness and heed President Lincoln's words by having "charity for all."

CHAPTER 17

EXPECTATIONS AND SENTENCING

Q. As a judge, what should courts expect from people, and how do you go about deciding criminal sentences? Thank you, Hailey

A. Hailey, courts expect people to be honest, well-behaved, and on time. Courts also expect people to give their best efforts to be responsible for themselves and their actions. This includes fulfilling the promises they make.

I use time in court to explain why we are gathered and what is expected from everyone. I also encourage questions and take time to answer them. When criminal defendants are unable to participate due to mental health or substance abuse issues, I order evaluations and try to help them regain their footing.

Lawyers who appear in my courtroom should be candid, prepared, and reasonable. They should be polite and on time. Fortunately, we are blessed with many courteous and talented local lawyers.

Now, let's focus on criminal sentencing. The five traditional objectives of sentencing are punishment, deterrence, incapacitation, rehabilitation, and restitution.

Punishment is self-explanatory. The goal of deterrence is to discourage defendants and others from committing future crimes. Incapacitation means defendants can't commit additional crimes in the community while they are locked up. Rehabilitation is the process of restoring someone to a useful and constructive place in society. Restitution means defendants must right the wrongs they directly caused by their crimes by making their victims as whole as possible.

As your county judge, I sentence defendants for misdemeanors. Many of the sentences I impose are plea agreements—this means the prosecutor, defense attorney, and defendant have already signed off on the terms. I don't participate in their negotiations, and my role is to either accept or reject their agreement. In contrast, I alone decide the terms of sentences when juries return guilty verdicts at trial, defendants enter open pleas, or defendants violate their probation.

Sentencing should be fair, merciful, and just. It's also important for the sentences of similar defendants to be consistent and proportionate.

Sentencing is not a power trip. I find it to be incredibly humbling because people's liberty and reputations are at stake. It's important for me to prepare and be deliberative, not emotional. I tend to give people the benefit of the doubt and don't adjudicate them guilty or impose jail time unless they've earned it and deserve it. That said, don't take me or any other judge lightly. Sooner or later, criminal misbehavior has consequences that leaves indelible marks.

County judges genuinely care about people and their communities. We strive to be fair, to help people resolve their differences, and to prevent them from progressing from misdemeanors to felonies.

CHAPTER 18

TWO-SIDED PANCAKES

Q. Judge Smith, why do plaintiffs and prosecutors always go first at trial? That does not seem fair to defendants. Thank you, Maria

A. Maria, before I answer your question, let's cover some essentials. Plaintiffs sue defendants in civil lawsuits, and prosecutors bring charges against defendants in criminal cases.

Although both sides take turns presenting opening statements, evidence, and closing arguments, plaintiffs and prosecutors present their cases first because they bear the burden of proof. This is not a matter of preferential treatment, but rather to determine if they can meet minimum evidentiary thresholds.

Unless plaintiffs and prosecutors prove that a factual basis exists to support their claims, judges will dismiss their cases mid-trial. Thus, requiring plaintiffs and prosecutors to go first at trial is fair, efficient, and cost-effective. Moreover, going second allows defendants to observe the cases against them and adjust their strategies accordingly.

One of our local mediators is fond of saying there's never been a pancake so thin that it didn't have two sides. This means there are two sides to every story, and we should give both sides a full opportunity to be heard before deciding cases. His metaphor mirrors the law.

When trials begin, judges give juries the "two-sided pancake" instruction: "You should not form any definite or fixed opinion on the merits of the case until you have heard all the evidence, the arguments of the lawyers, and the Court's instructions on the law."

Given the back-and-forth nature of trials, both parties get an equal opportunity to present their cases, and neither side goes unchallenged. Juries decide factual issues based on the sworn testimony of witnesses and items admitted into evidence, such as documents, photographs, murder weapons, etc. Generally, the lawyer calling a witness can ask open-ended non-leading questions. This is called direct examination. For example:

Q. Did you see the car accident?
Q. Which car had the right-of-way to drive through the intersection?

In contrast, the opposing lawyer can ask the witness leading questions that suggest the desired answer. This is called cross-examination. For example:

Q. You told Deputy Hatcher that the accident was entirely

Ms. Baker's fault, didn't you?
Q. And that's because you saw her run a steady red-light, correct?

After both sides have finished presenting evidence, the lawyers sum up their cases in closing arguments. Next, the Court delivers its final instructions on the law, and the jury deliberates until it reaches a unanimous verdict or becomes deadlocked.

Maria, I hope this helps.

CHAPTER 19

APPOINTED AND ELECTED JUDGES

Q. Judge Smith, how did you become a judge, and what do you like the most about your job? — Kendra

A. Kendra, let's cover how people become judges and then focus on my job.

Federal judges are nominated by the president, confirmed by the United States Senate, and appointed for life. Federal judges can choose to retire, but no one can force them out if they're competent and well-behaved.

Lifetime appointments insulate federal judges from the politics of the day. They can follow the rule of law, even when doing so is unpopular, without having to worry about losing their jobs. This check and balance protects the judicial branch from rank politics and the tyranny of the mob. A downside to lifetime appointments is that the people must endure poor performers for a long time.

In comparison, state trial judges obtain their offices by appointment or election, and state appellate judges obtain their offices by appointment only. State court appointments follow a two-step process to fill open seats arising from an incumbent's promotion, retirement, death, or removal from office.

A "judicial nominating committee" exists for each state court. Open seats are publicly noticed, and all eligible lawyers are invited to apply. After the judicial nominating committee vets and interviews applicants, it refers 3 to 6 names to the governor for consideration. The governor appoints new judges from the "short lists" he receives from judicial nominating committees.

State judges appointed to fill open seats must stand for election or retention. The trial judges serving on the circuit and county benches face contested elections against other candidates. The appellate judges serving on the district courts of appeal and the state Supreme Court face yes/no retention elections. All state judges are elected or retained to serve six-year terms.

Unlike federal judges, state judges have a mandatory retirement age, and effective July 1, 2019, they must retire by their 75th birthdays. State court judges who misbehave can be impeached by the Florida Senate, removed from office by the state Supreme Court, or voted out of office by the people.

Electing or retaining state judges allows the people to choose who will serve them in these positions. A downside to electing judges is that those facing close elections may be tempted succumb to political pressures rather than following the rule of law. Thus, integrity matters.

I became a county judge by appointment and the people of Leon County elected me to serve a six-year term. The thing I enjoy most is having daily contact with regular people and helping them resolve their cases. I love my job and am grateful for the opportunity to serve you.

Keep Judge
SMITH
Leon County Judge, Seat 2
ElectJudgeSmith.com

CHAPTER 20

WHEN DUTY CONFLICTS WITH FAITH

Q. Judge Smith, how do elected officials balance conflicts between their public duties and their personal religious beliefs? Thank you, Maria

A. Maria, let's begin by covering the basic civics and legal principles involved, and then I'll explain how I balance conflicts.

When it comes to my job, I can't simply do as I please. Consider how arrogant and selfish it would be for me, or any other judge, to ignore the collective wisdom and rightful authority of Congress, the legislature, and/or the appellate courts and apply our personal religious beliefs to cases. Here's why.

County judges aren't supposed to make public policy or try to influence it. That power lies exclusively with Congress and the state legislature. Instead, I, like my fellow county judges throughout the state, swore an oath to follow and apply the laws of our nation and our state.

Trial judges work alone and are required to make quick and intuitive decisions. We are guided by our life experience, knowledge of the law, and input from competing parties and lawyers. Some decisions are close calls, and like all humans, sometimes we err. Fortunately, our decisions can be appealed.

In contrast, most appellate decisions are made by panels of three or more judges, who each reflectively review trial transcripts and the applicable law. Their combined efforts promote consistency, predictability, and getting cases right. Written appellate decisions provide clarity and direction for trial judges, lawyers, and society.

As a trial judge, I am duty-bound to follow appellate decisions regarding school prayer, the separation of church and state, and other potentially controversial issues. These decisions are the binding authority, and my personal beliefs as a Christian are irrelevant to fulfilling my job duties. If there is ever a conflict between the two, I must and will follow the law. Period.

Now, let's focus on the bigger picture. We are a nation and state of laws—not of men or women. This means no one is above the law, and the law applies equally to everyone, regardless of rank, position, or status.

Like me, every elected official swears an oath to protect, defend, and support the constitutions, and secular laws of the nation and of their states. The elected officials responsible for making public policy can advocate wholesale changes to the law, enact new laws, and modify existing ones. Indeed, that's their role. Notwithstanding, anyone who dislikes the existing law still must follow it or face the consequences. That's just the way it is.

CHAPTER 21
THE SOUND OF SILENCE

Q. Judge Smith, why don't judges comment on political issues, and how do judges manage heavy caseloads? Thank you, Alvin

A. Alvin, you've asked two excellent questions. Our state constitution deliberately divides the powers of government among the legislative, executive, and judicial branches. The legislature establishes the public policy, the executive enforces the law, and the judiciary interprets and follows the law.

Judges don't make or influence public policy. Although we zealously protect your free speech rights, we voluntarily surrender some of our own free speech rights. Why? Because if we openly chose sides on partisan issues, it would undermine the people's confidence in our ability to decide cases on the merits.

The reality is that judges vote and have political preferences. However, we are honor-bound to follow the law, and render fair and impartial decisions.

So, how do judges stay non-partisan and above the fray? We take "political vows of silence." We don't attend partisan functions, solicit or accept endorsements from political parties, or endorse candidates. Nor do we raise money or ask for political contributions.

Of course, the ultimate irony is that getting appointed, elected, or re-elected to the bench involves politics! Trial judges stand for contested elections, and appellate judges stand for retention. Thus, voters decide all of our fates. However, no mudslinging is allowed, and all other politics are off-limits.

Sometimes, judges are involuntarily silent. Last month, I had a bad case of laryngitis. Lawyer jokes aside, judges do a lot of talking. So, what does a mute judge do? I spent my downtime reading, writing, and thinking. Do you want to know my big takeaway? Some redundancies are necessary for good government!

Judges serve on bar committees, take on leadership positions, and are active in our communities. We teach, take judicial training, and have vacation and sick days. We are cross-trained to fill in for each other as needed. Trial judges manage heavy caseloads by working as individuals and as interchangeable team members.

Having experienced and available judges allows us to schedule more trials and move our dockets efficiently. When I had laryngitis, other judges covered my dockets, and the public continued to be well-served. Likewise, I cover hearings and trials for other judges, too. Often, justice delayed is justice denied, and having trial judges at the ready benefits Floridians and the state's economy.

Florida makes efficient use of its judicial resources, spending less than 1% of its annual budget on the state's judicial branch. The state employs 4.5 trial judges per 100,000 residents, compared to the national average of 6.6 trial judges per 100,000 residents.

Alvin, now you know why judges stay out of politics and how we handle heavy caseloads.

CHAPTER 22

LIKE PEAS AND CARROTS

Although law enforcement officers and trial judges play important but different roles, they share many common objectives. Let's compare the two.

Law enforcement officers are responsible for serving the public and keeping the peace. They are the thin blue line that shields us from chaos and anarchy. These men and women often deal with people at their worst and must be skilled at diffusing volatile situations. You'd be surprised at how many hours law enforcement officers spend protecting and helping people. They patrol neighborhoods, check up on the wellbeing of others, and protect vulnerable people from predators.

Law enforcement officers also investigate crimes and establish probable cause for arrests and search warrants. They investigate and report relevant facts, which tend to incriminate or exonerate. Like lawyers, they must have a working knowledge of criminal law, the Fourth, Fifth, and Sixth Amendments, and the current case law.

Law enforcement officers' jobs aren't easy, nor are they meant to be. They embody the power of the state, and a reliable and trusted police force is vital to the continued success of a free people.

Trial judges are responsible for ensuring due process of law, faithfully following the rule of law, and balancing mercy and justice. Being a trial judge is analogous to being the doctor at a Mobile Army Surgical Hospital (think the M*A*S*H 4077 unit in the Korean War). Like those doctors, trial judges don't control the flow of bodies and they also must perform triage. They're also confronted by people at their worst and are required to diffuse volatile situations. Consider this: Half of the parties in contested cases will be unhappy with the final judgments that are rendered. Trial judges' jobs aren't easy either, nor are they meant to be.

Good trial judges treat people with dignity and respect. They prepare, explain, listen intently, and render thoughtful, fair, and prompt rulings. By fulfilling their duties, they also protect people from bullies, tyrants, and injustice.

Any abuse of power or dereliction of duty by law enforcement officers or trial judges weakens the rule of law. Corruption or incompetence by either undermines the people's trust in their government. Justice should also be visible; good conduct and transparency by law enforcement officers and judges always matter because any appearance of impropriety will also erode the public's trust.

My experience is that people want to understand and believe in their government, but they sometimes struggle to do so. As public servants, law enforcement officers and trial judges should regularly explain their roles to the people and set an expectation of civility, compassion, and consequences. People are also more likely to hear this message if it's delivered with kindness and humility.

CHAPTER 23

MERRY CHRISTMAS FROM THE LEON COUNTY JAIL

There are certain jobs that require people to work on holidays. If asked to identify them, you'd probably list doctors, law enforcement, and Waffle House employees. It might surprise you to know that judges work holidays, weekends, and evenings too, and at least one of us is on call no matter the day of the year.

I'm duty judge on Christmas Eve. During my shift, I'll cover juvenile hearings and first appearances for Leon, Franklin, Gadsden, Jefferson, Liberty and Wakulla counties.

It's my routine to prepare for trials and hearings at least a day in advance. This includes working on weekends. That's not possible with first appearances because the materials I'll need to review will not be available until shortly before the hearings start.

For kicks, let's run through my day. Tomorrow morning my alarm clock will sound off at 6 a.m., which will give me just enough time to rush my morning routine and make it to the courthouse by 7 a.m. By then, the first appearance docket will be available for the Leon County cases, and I'll spend the next 75 minutes reviewing 200-500 pages of case-related material.

No doubt that sounds harder and more intimidating than it is. I'm no speed reader, but after logging 31 years as a trial lawyer, general counsel, and county judge, I know what to focus on and why. If I don't have time to read everything before the hearings start, I'll finish my review during the hearings.

By 8:15, I'll drive to the Juvenile Detention Center to field and cover the juvenile cases for the day. This typically takes no more than an hour. As soon as I finish, I'll drive to the Leon County Jail to conduct first appearances for the defendants there. That typically takes two to four hours, depending on the volume and complexity of the cases.

After I finish handling the Leon County cases, I'll review the paperwork that has been faxed in for first appearances in Franklin, Gadsden, Jefferson, Liberty and Wakulla counties. The out-of-county hearings will be conducted by jail-to-jail audio/video feed.

Anyone who is arrested has the right to see a judge within 24 hours of being booked into the jail. The purpose of first appearance is to:

1) advise the defendant of his rights;

2) determine whether to appoint a public defender;

3) explain the criminal charge(s) against him;

4) review the probable cause affidavit and determine whether there was a factual and legal basis for the arrest;

5) hear the arguments of counsel; and

6) set any pre-trial release conditions.

Because defendants are presumed innocent, the law favors their pretrial release. Judges may impose pretrial release conditions on defendants who are higher risks for not showing up at hearings. Judges may also impose pretrial release conditions on defendants who are dangerous to themselves, their victims, or the public. The purpose of conditions is to assure defendants' attendance and promote safety.

Now, behave, or I'll be wishing you a Merry Christmas from the Leon County Jail!

PART III

BEING THE JURY

CHAPTER 24

FAIR AND IMPARTIAL JURIES

Q. How does the justice system work to ensure that the juries sitting on criminal cases are fair and impartial to both sides?
— Carol

A. Carol, each criminal defendant has the right to a trial by an impartial jury, and the clerk of court and the trial court work hard to ensure that occurs. Now, let's cover how jurors are assembled, qualified, and selected.

<u>Random Pools of Jurors</u>

Approximately 184,000 Leon County residents are eligible for jury service, and multiple jury trials are held at the courthouse weekly. Four weeks out, the jury pool for a trial week is randomly selected by a computer algorithm, which eliminates the risk of human bias. During 2018, 38,111 residents of Leon County were summonsed and approximately 22,867 of them served.

Qualification

When a jury pool is assembled, a judge puts them under oath and confirms they meet the minimum statutory qualifications. Prospective jurors can serve if they: 1) are at least 18 years old; 2) are citizens of the United States; 3) reside in the county; and 4) have driver's licenses or identification cards issued by the State or provide affidavits attesting to their eligibility.

Random Assignment

After prospective jurors have been qualified, a computer algorithm randomly seats them in sequential order.

Selection Process

After prospective jurors have been seated and instructed by the court, they answer questions and provide basic information about themselves. Lawyers eliminate prospective jurors from service by exercising "for cause" and "peremptory" strikes.

For-Cause Strikes

A prospective juror can't serve if he or she has a bias or prejudice for or against a party. Each party can assert an unlimited number of challenges for cause. Let's consider two examples.

In a driving-while-impaired case, a prospective juror whose child was killed by a drunk driver might be struck for cause. Likewise, in a grand theft case, a prospective juror whose wife was convicted of a crime by the same prosecuting attorney might be struck for cause.

Peremptory Strikes and Challenges

Each party may strike a set number of prospective jurors from serving without having to give any reason for doing so. One notable exception applies. A party may not eliminate a juror based solely on race, ethnicity, or gender. If challenged, the lawyer must provide a neutral explanation that is supported by the record and found to be genuine by the trial judge.

Selection

Jury selection is open to the public. The process is recorded, preserved, and subject to appeal. Every participant, including the trial judge, is accountable. Each juror promises under oath to be fair and impartial, and to follow the court's instructions on the law. Following this process safeguards constitutional rights and produces fair and impartial juries.

CHAPTER 25

MY PATRIOTIC, FLAG-WAVING, JURY SERVICE SPEECH

Q. Judge Smith, I've heard you talk about the importance of jury service. Can you cover that topic with your readers? Thank you, Ken

A. Ken, nothing is more American than our jury system, and every time I qualify jurors, I give them my patriotic, flag-waving jury service speech. To set the mood, imagine someone in the background is playing "Yankee Doodle" on a flute. Here goes:

Let's talk about the elephant in the room.

You probably weren't thrilled to be called for jury service. I get it. You're busy and have other things to do. However, let's talk about the importance of jury service.

We fought and won the Revolutionary War partially because the British legal system was unfair to us. People died and blood has been spilt to earn you this privilege.

In colonial days, judges were appointed by the King. They were beholden to the King and could be replaced by the King. They served the Crown, not the people, and they had no incentive to do right by the people.

Colonial defendants didn't enjoy the rights we take for granted. They didn't have the right to jury trials or the right to the assistance of counsel. They had no right against self-incrimination and could be forced to testify. If they remained silent, their silence could be used against them.

British authorities didn't have to tell colonial defendants what they were accused of and people languished in jails under cruel conditions. People and their property could be searched and seized without good cause and without the review and approval of an independent judge. If a colonist was acquitted at trial and the Crown didn't like the result, the colonist could be re-tried for the same offense.

These British abuses were so chronic that our Founders separated the powers of government and instituted a system of checks and balances to prevent any person or branch from accumulating too much power.

Our Founders understood human nature and believed that "absolute power corrupts absolutely." They structured our government to protect us from tyrants.

Trials by juries allow regular people, randomly selected from the community, to hear evidence and decide the facts of cases. Juries protect us from the tyranny of appointed and elected officials, religious figures, and the mob mentality. The role juries play in our system of justice is so important that it is guaranteed by the Constitution.

Now, let's make it personal. Suppose, God forbid, that you or a loved one were on trial today. Your fate or their fate would depend on a group of strangers who didn't want to be here. Let that sink in for a moment.

Our goal is to pick jurors who'll be fair and impartial to both sides and who will fulfill their promises to follow the law. So please be honest and patient. Thank you, and God bless you.

CHAPTER 26

WHAT JURIES DON'T HEAR AT TRIAL

Q. Judge Smith, what do judges and lawyers talk about when they huddle, and why aren't jurors allowed to listen in? — Pat

A. Pat, a jury must base its verdict solely on the evidence admitted at trial, in accordance with the court's instructions on the law. That objective becomes harder to accomplish if jurors are exposed to inadmissible evidence and faulty legal arguments.

Judges and lawyers hold sidebar conversations and conduct hearings apart from juries to prevent them from being tainted by what they are not supposed to hear. Juries are instructed not to speculate about what is discussed outside of their presence, and as a result, less errors and mistrials occur.

Like a magician revealing his trick, I'll share with you what goes on behind the scenes. Sidebar conversations and hearings that exclude juries usually involve one or more of these topics:

1. Evidence

The Florida Legislature enacted an evidence code, which serves as a filter. The judge sustains or overrules lawyers' objections regarding evidence.

2. Pre-Trial Rulings

Lawyers can obtain pre-trial rulings about the validity of traffic stops, the legality of searches and seizures, or the admissibility of evidence. During trial, some pre-trial rulings need to be modified or reconsidered.

3. Expert Witnesses

The judge and lawyers conduct hearings about the qualifications of expert witnesses and any limitations that will be placed on the scope of their testimonies.

4. Mistrials

A lawyer or witness may say or do something that causes a mistrial. If so, the judge and lawyers discuss if a mistrial can be avoided by having the judge instruct the jury to disregard the transgression.

5. Motions for Judgment of Acquittal

The State must provide evidence for each element of a charged crime. After the State rests its case, the defense can test whether the State satisfied this requirement by moving for a judgment of acquittal. The judge hears and decides this motion while the jury is out on break.

6. The Defendant's Right Against Self-Incrimination

After the State rests, the defendant must decide whether to testify or not. The defendant talks to his lawyer in private and then informs the court.

7. The Defendant's Decision About Putting on a Case

After the State rests, the defense must decide whether to call any witnesses.

8. Scheduling and Logistics

Some sidebar conversations cover timing issues and logistics, such as taking witnesses out of sequence or when to break for lunch.

9. Final Jury Instructions

The judge and lawyers work together to finalize the jury instructions and verdict form that will be read to the jury.

Now you know what judges and lawyers talk about when jurors aren't allowed to listen in. Following this process safeguards constitutional rights and promotes fair trials.

CHAPTER 27

SUNSHINE AND SEQUESTRATION

Q. Judge Smith, I was a witness in a criminal case. The morning of the trial, the judge told me to leave the courtroom and return when it was time for me to testify. I spent the next two hours waiting in the hallway before being called to testify. I thought courtrooms were public forums. Why did I have to leave? — Katie

A. Katie, Florida is known as the "Sunshine State" for two reasons. First, it's a vacation wonderland and people flock to our sunny beaches. Second, the public policy of our state mandates open and transparent government. To quote a song, "Let the Sunshine In!"

Our state's courtrooms are public forums that are open to the public and the media. However, having an open and transparent government is not the state's only policy objective. Florida also provides people, businesses, and organizations with fair trials, and the law works to balance both objectives.

Pleadings, motions, court orders, and other papers filed in civil and criminal cases are public records, and they can be read and copied by anyone. Trials and court hearings are generally open to the public, too. Otherwise, people would have less confidence that our courts are fair and impartial.

The law imposes some exceptions to everyone having complete access to every government record or public forum. Let's cover two quick examples, including the one that affected you.

Trial judges have the authority to control their courtrooms. When people are disruptive and refuse to behave, judges will have them removed from their courtrooms.

On the other hand, you were instructed to leave the courtroom until it was time for your testimony because of the rule of sequestration.

Fact witnesses are supposed to testify about what they know firsthand. This typically involves something they directly observed or experienced through one or more of their five senses (seeing, hearing, smelling, touching, or tasting). Generally, witnesses do not testify about what they overheard someone else say (objection – hearsay – sustained!).

The rule of sequestration prevents fact witnesses from overhearing other witnesses' testimony. This ensures they aren't influenced by what others say, restricting their testimony to what they know.

Usually, the rule of sequestration is invoked before a trial begins. In my courtroom, I explain to the affected witnesses what the rule is and its purpose. When witnesses have finished testifying, I tell them they are free to go, or remain and observe.

The law carefully and thoughtfully balances the need to allow people to observe justice, warts and all, and to ensure all parties receive fair and impartial trials. In this sense, Florida is the envy of the world. Our state and local governments are open and transparent. Our courts dispense fair and impartial justice. And let's not forget our sunny beaches! I invite you to visit your county courthouse and a Florida beach to see for yourself.

CHAPTER 28

ANNIVERSARIES AND AFFIRMATIONS

Time flies when you're having fun! For the past two years (2018-2019), I've published this column every other Sunday. I'm grateful to the *Tallahassee Democrat* for providing me with a platform to discuss civics, law, and the administration of justice. I'd also like to thank my readers for their questions and kind words. Now, let's turn our attention to oaths.

Q. Judge Smith, as a practicing Christian, my religious beliefs forbid me from swearing oaths. Can a court compel me to take an oath? Will my refusal prevent me from testifying or serving as a juror? — Anne

A. Anne, James 5:12 reads, "…do not swear, either by heaven or by earth or with any other oath; but your yes is to be yes, and your no, no…."

The First Amendment protects your right to freedom of religion from interference by the government. Thus, no court will compel you to swear an oath.

Now, think of a trial as a search for truth. Due process requires notice, the opportunity to be heard, fairness, and conformity with the law. The culmination leads to a jury verdict on the merits.

Fairness requires prospective jurors to be candid and forthright during jury selection. If chosen, they must follow the court's jury instructions. Decisions on the merits must be based on the evidence, and thus witnesses have a duty to be completely truthful. Witnesses are asked to swear oaths to tell the whole truth to emphasize the solemnity of the occasion, their duty to be honest, and the consequences of lying.

As an alternative to swearing an oath, you can instead affirm that you will "tell the truth, the whole truth and nothing but the truth." Merely affirming that you will be truthful is consistent with James 5:12 and it satisfies the court's need to promote truth. Taking that action will allow you to testify or serve as a juror. I hope this helps.

Q. Judge Smith, I am in fourth grade. Why do people have to raise their right hands to testify? Thank you, Billy
A. Billy, witnesses are told to raise their right hands when oaths are administered because of long-standing tradition. Before electricity, computers, and modern record-keeping, this tradition had a more practical but dire reason.

As early as medieval times, people convicted of crimes of dishonesty were punished by having the palms of their right hands branded with hot irons. OUCH! The scars on their right palms served notice that they were convicted felons, which was obvious to everyone when they raised their right hands to testify. Since the foundation of our Republic, the Eighth Amendment has prohibited the government from imposing "cruel and unusual" punishments, including branding.

Billy, our history is full of interesting people and stories. If you stay curious and study history, you'll be highly entertained.

PART IV

ANSWERS TO BASIC LEGAL QUESTIONS

CHAPTER 29

LINCOLN'S LOGIC

Q. Judge Smith, my friend John is charged with a crime. John wants to defend himself. Can he, and should he? Thank you, Sarah

A. Sarah, you asked two excellent questions. John may be allowed to defend himself, but it will depend on the circumstances.

The Sixth Amendment guarantees criminal defendants a right to counsel. Given the high stakes involved, most people do not want to represent themselves, and the mere thought of it strikes terror into their hearts. Many are afraid of public speaking, and most lack legal training and courtroom experience.

A criminal defendant rarely opts to represent himself. In response, the court conducts a hearing with the defendant and confirms that he or she is thinking clearly and understands the perils of self-representation. The charges, the range of sentences, and potential pitfalls are discussed.

Before becoming our 16th President, Abraham Lincoln was a highly successful trial lawyer. He observed that "a lawyer who represents himself has a fool for a client." Lincoln's observation is short, pithy, and spot-on! Here's why. Most people, including lawyers, are emotional and defensive when facing a personal crisis. Even if they understand the law, legal procedure and evidence, they tend to be emotional instead of logical. I can't think of a single example where a lawyer or judge accused of a crime opted to defend himself or herself at trial. That's because lawyers and judges understand the value of bringing another advocate's perspective, logic, and calmness to the battle.

Imagine, if you will, that a courtroom is a minefield. The prosecutor, knowing where bombs are buried, has the home field advantage. The layman, who goes it alone, doesn't know where it's safe to step. One false step and KABOOM!

As a judge, I can't ignore a criminal defendant's request to represent himself simply because I think he is making a mistake. He can waive his right to counsel if that decision is knowing, voluntary, and informed.

Now, let's focus on your friend John. Should he represent himself? Probably not. Defendants who represent themselves often lose winnable cases.

Do you remember the 1965-1968 television series "Lost in Space"? In it, when Will Robinson faced danger, the robot flailed his arms wildly and shouted, "Danger, Will Robinson,

Danger!" It'd help if the "Lost in Space" robot would provide the same danger warning to criminal defendants who opt to defend themselves.

CHAPTER 30

SHE SLASHED A HOLE IN ALL FOUR TIRES

Q. Judge Smith, last weekend my favorite niece was arrested for "criminal mischief." What does that mean, and how serious is the charge? Sincerely, a mystified Uncle Jimmy

A. Uncle Jimmy, you are mystified because the label is misleading. "Mischief" sounds like a good-natured prankster having some harmless fun. However, "criminal mischief" occurs when someone "willfully and maliciously" injures or damages the property of another. It includes acts of vandalism and graffiti.

Criminal mischief cases always remind me of Carrie Underwood's song "Before He Cheats." My daughter is home from college this summer, and much to her annoyance, I have whistled that tune all afternoon. It could have been worse—I could have sung it. The lyrics of "Before He Cheats" describe a textbook case of criminal mischief. Consider these lines from the song:

"I dug my key into the side of his pretty little souped-up four-wheel drive [vandalism / damage];

"Carved my name into his leather seats [vandalism / damage];

"I took a Louisville Slugger to both headlights [property damage];

"Slashed a hole in all four tires [property damage];

"Maybe next time he'll think before he cheats [motive: anger, revenge]."

Criminal mischief can be a crime of jealousy, spitefulness, or even revenge. For example, Bob is dating Sally but suspects she might be seeing someone else on the side. Bob "gets even" by pouring bleach on Sally's wardrobe or throwing a brick through the front windshield of her car. Bob is then charged with criminal mischief. Don't be like Bob.

Uncle Jimmy, you also asked about the seriousness of the crime. If the alleged property damage is $200 or less, the defendant can be charged with a second-degree misdemeanor, which is punishable by up to 60 days in the county jail, a $500 fine, court costs, and payment of restitution to make the victim whole.

If the alleged property damage is greater than $200 but does not exceed $1,000, the defendant can be charged with a first-degree misdemeanor, which is punishable by up to a year in the county jail, a $1,000 fine, court costs, and restitution.

If the alleged property damage exceeds $1,000, the defendant can be charged with a third-degree felony, which is punishable by up to five years in state prison, a $5,000 fine, court costs, and restitution.

Depending on her circumstances, the charge your niece faces could be minor or quite serious. She would be well advised to maintain her Fifth Amendment right against self-incrimination and not discuss the facts of her case with anyone other than her attorney—not even a favorite uncle.

CHAPTER 31

CAESAR AND GOLLUM EXPLAIN LATIN

Q. Judge Smith, what are summonses and subpoenas? Thank you, Cheryl

A. Cheryl, I'm glad you don't know about summonses and subpoenas from personal experience! Part of my job as your county judge is to explain the law, including unfamiliar legal terms. Let's tackle these two.

Both *summons* and *subpoena* are Latin words (think "Julius Caesar" Latin, not "Jennifer Lopez" Latin). We inherited them from the English common law, and their Latin origins explain why the singular and plural forms of both words sound odd and have goofy spellings.

The plural of *summons* is *summonses.* Imagine in "The Lord of the Rings" if Gollum, who always spoke in plurals, had sued Bilbo Baggins for the return of his ring. He would have said, "We serves the summonses on the Bagginses!"

A summons is used to tell someone something. Prospective jurors are served with summonses to tell them they have jury duty. Civil defendants are served with summonses and plaintiffs' complaints to tell them that they have been sued and what actions they must take to defend themselves and avoid losing by default. Anyone served with a summons should read it carefully and be mindful of key dates and deadlines. Time is of the essence, and civil defendants should seek immediate legal advice.

People with liability insurance should promptly provide copies of summonses and lawsuits to their insurance agents and insurance companies. If a defendant's claim is covered, the insurance company will provide a defense and pay damages.

Subpoenas are court orders that require witnesses to show up and testify at depositions, hearings, or trials. Subpoenas are also court orders that require people, businesses, or organizations to produce things (tangible items) for inspection, or information for copying or inspection. The word subpoena literally means "under penalty," and anyone who ignores a subpoena may face penalties, such as paying a fine, paying attorney fees, and/or spending time in jail.

People served with subpoenas who have reason to believe they are being targeted for civil liability lawsuits or criminal prosecution should immediately seek legal advice and/or representation. The same goes for witnesses who do not have entirely clear consciences.

Parties should serve subpoenas on key witnesses to ensure they testify at trial. Likewise, parties should subpoena records from others to gather proof. People lose winnable cases every day because they don't line up key witnesses and prove key facts.

Cheryl, I hope this explanation helps!

CHAPTER 32

MARSHAL DILLON TO THE RESCUE

Q. Judge Smith, what is the difference between the police and the sheriff, and what is their authority for making arrests? Thank you, Charles

A. Charles, police officers are employed by city governments, and sheriffs and their deputies are employed by county governments. So, police officers serve and protect people and property within their cities, and sheriffs and their deputies serve and protect people and property within their counties.

Let's apply that to the City of Tallahassee and Leon County. Generally, our local police officers' jurisdiction is confined to the city limits, and they do not police the unincorporated areas of the county. However, the sheriff's jurisdiction covers the entire county, which includes the City of Tallahassee. As a result, the jurisdictions of the Tallahassee Police Department and the Leon County Sheriff's Office overlap within the city limits.

There are other noteworthy differences between the two. The city hires its chief of police, who answers directly to the city manager and/or to our elected city officials. In contrast, the sheriff is an independently elected constitutional officer who answers directly to the voters. The sheriff operates the county jail and provides security for both county courthouses.

Charles, you also asked about the source of a law enforcement officer's authority to make arrests. The answer is the law.

Remember the cowboy movies and western series you watched as a kid? Outlaws did whatever they wanted without regard to others. They controlled the roads, towns, and outposts until U.S. Marshal Matt Dillon of Dodge City rode in and saved the day. To combat lawlessness and protect us from criminals, the government provides security through law enforcement.

Think of government as a social contract. People want and need protection from outlaws. In response, our elected officials at the federal, state, and local levels have enacted laws authorizing government to keep the peace by exercising "police power," which includes making lawful arrests. In exchange, each one of us is subject to the law and expected to follow the law. Now, let's discuss the usual scenarios in which law enforcement officers make arrests.

Law enforcement officers make "on-view arrests" if they observe someone commit a crime or when, during the course of an on-the-scene investigation, they determine there is "probable cause" that the arrestee committed a crime. An "on-view arrest" might also occur during the execution of a search warrant.

As part of their jobs, law enforcement officers encounter people they arrest because of unresolved arrest warrants. When that happens, a judge has already found "probable cause" for the arrest and issued the warrant. These warrants may be local, from another county or state, or from the federal government.

If someone violates the conditions of their probation, they are subject to arrest. Likewise, someone may be arrested if they violate the terms of their pre-trial release. For example, the court will order a defendant charged with a domestic battery to have no further contact with the victim. If the defendant violates the no-contact order, he will be re-arrested. Courts also issue bench warrants for the arrest of criminal defendants who fail to appear at scheduled and noticed hearings, jury selections, and trials.

CHAPTER 33

JOBS, WELFARE, OR CRIME

Q. Judge Smith, I volunteer time with a church group that helps people find jobs. One of the women I am trying to place has a felony conviction for stealing a pair of shoes. This is her only felony conviction! Help me understand why such an insignificant crime was classified as a felony? Respectfully, Afra

A. Afra, thank you for helping unemployed people find jobs. The time you spend helping them is invaluable.

Long-term unemployment generates poverty and widespread misery. It crushes souls. Unemployment is also a leading cause of recidivism, which happens when former felons reoffend and must return to prison. Anecdotally, nine out of 10 defendants I see at first appearance are chronically unemployed.

Think about it. Without jobs, unemployed adults and their families must subsist on government support. Some chronically unemployed people turn to crime for additional income.

Others commit crimes to vent frustration over their inability to earn money or as a cure for boredom.

We need to help former felons successfully reintegrate back into society. Their families and children are depending on them, and to quote President Reagan, "the best social program is a job."

Now, to your question: why was stealing a pair of shoes classified as a felony? Let's begin by covering the essential civics to provide the context.

The powers of the government are divided among three co-equal branches and it is the legislature that establishes the state's policy. Statutes enacted by the legislature put everyone on notice of which acts, or omissions, are crimes. Likewise, by statutes, the legislature establishes the seriousness, and the sentencing exposure, for each crime. The legislature classifies less serious crimes as misdemeanors and more serious crimes as felonies.

The criminal classification and sentencing exposure for a theft charge depends on two things: 1) the value of the property taken; and 2) the number of times a defendant has previously been convicted of theft.

The legislature has established the property value thresholds for theft charges. A defendant charged with stealing property valued at $750 or less will be charged with a misdemeanor. A defendant charged with taking property valued at more than $750 will be charged with a felony.

A new charge of theft against a defendant who has already been convicted of theft two or more times will be charged as a felony, regardless of the value of the property taken. The policy objective for enhancing criminal charges based on prior convictions is to promote deterrence.

Afra, the lady you are helping wasn't convicted of felony theft because of the value of the shoes she stole. Rather, she was convicted of felony theft because she already had two prior theft convictions. I hope my explanation helps.

CHAPTER 34

JUGGLING CHAINSAWS

Q. Judge Smith, does bad conduct expose a person to criminal prosecution, civil liability, or both? Just asking for a friend! —Stan

A. Stan, bad conduct can expose someone to both. Let's begin by comparing criminal and civil law. The state enacts and enforces criminal laws to protect the public and keep the peace. Only the state may charge and prosecute crimes. Civil laws provide remedies to peacefully resolve disputes between private parties. Typically, civil cases involve claims to establish liability and damages. They can also cover property disputes, injunctions, and family matters.

Sometimes the same conduct can expose a person to criminal prosecution and civil liability. You may recall the State of California prosecuting O. J. Simpson for two murders and the victims' families suing him for "wrongful death." Defending criminal and civil cases arising out of the same fact pattern is complicated, and it is as dangerous as juggling chainsaws! I know from my days as trial lawyer, and I still have the scars to prove it.

Let's use an example to show how criminal and civil cases can arise from the same fact pattern. Criminal battery and civil battery are similar, except they involve different parties and standards of proof.

Civil Lawsuit for Battery

Civil battery happens when someone intentionally makes a harmful or offensive contact with another person without the victim's consent, and it causes the victim to suffer damages. Typically, battery involves uninvited hitting or groping.

George's favorite football team is the Los Angeles Rams. Recently, while watching the Super Bowl at a local bar, George sucker-punched a New England Patriots fan and broke his jaw. The punch was unprovoked and captured by the bar's video surveillance camera.

The victim sues George for the intentional tort of battery. To win at trial, he must prove by the greater weight of the evidence that George intentionally caused him harmful contact and that he suffered damages.

The victim has a straightforward case. Being punched is a harmful contact. His claim for damages includes reimbursement for his medical expenses, and pain and suffering.

George has assets. That's fortunate, too, because liability insurance covers negligence, but it doesn't cover intentional acts.

To settle the lawsuit, George, who recently paid cash for his dream car, signs the title over to the victim.

Criminal Prosecution for Battery

The state charges George with criminal battery. To win at trial, the state must prove beyond a reasonable doubt that George either struck the victim against his will or intentionally caused him bodily harm. If convicted, George faces up to one year in the county jail, a $1,000 fine, and he might be ordered to pay restitution. Given the facts, George will either take a plea or bear the risk of a jury returning a guilty verdict.

Seek Legal Advice

Stan, people facing prosecution and/or civil liability should keep quiet about the cases against them and immediately consult lawyers for advice. After all, juggling chainsaws is a job best left to professionals.

CHAPTER 35

STAND AND BE COUNTED

Q. Judge Smith, what is an arraignment? Thank you, Lacey

A. Lacey, the word *arraign* is a verb that originated in England sometime in the late 1200s. Over time it has come to mean bringing defendants before courts, reading out the criminal charges against them, and having them answer the charges. Criminal charges must be specific enough to inform defendants what they are accused of and to prevent them from being charged multiple times for the same crimes. Our Founders believed arraignments were important enough to include an arraignment clause in the Sixth Amendment.

Today, some defendants are arrested, booked into the county jail, and held for a first appearance with a judge. Other defendants are provided with notices to attend arraignment hearings. An arraignment is the court hearing where a criminal defendant enters his or her initial plea of not guilty, no contest, or guilty.

At arraignments, judges protect defendants by explaining the purpose of the hearing and their fundamental rights. Judges explain the wisdom of pleading not guilty, the Fifth Amendment right against self-incrimination, and the Sixth Amendment right to counsel. If defendants can't afford counsel, courts appoint publicly funded lawyers to defend them.

Judges emphasize that defendants are not required to prove their innocence. Rather, the prosecutors bear the burden of proving the defendants' guilt beyond a reasonable doubt to impartial juries.

Pleading not guilty is an outright denial of all charges. This is a "safe harbor" plea and can be changed later. Defendants who have any doubts about what they should do are advised to plead not guilty.

Pleading no contest is neither an admission nor a denial of guilt. Instead, pleading no contest is a decision not to further contest the charges. Defendants plead no contest at arraignment to accept the prosecutors' plea offers. Typically, courts will accept plea agreements if the defendants understand the rights they are giving up and what they are getting in exchange. Their decisions to accept plea agreements must be made knowingly, voluntarily, and freely.

Pleading guilty is a confession and an admission of guilt. Depending on the facts, guilty pleas may expose criminal defendants to civil liability or other unintended consequences. Thus, defendants should always get legal advice before pleading guilty.

You can imagine how inefficient courts would be if people could skip scheduled hearings without any consequences. To avoid this chaos, defendants are informed they must attend their arraignments and other hearings or face arrest and possible detention for "failing to appear."

An ounce of prevention is worth a pound of cure. When in doubt, people should get legal advice to ensure they understand their rights and the consequences of their actions. Lacey, I hope this helps.

CHAPTER 36

OSTRICHES AND BLABBERMOUTHS LOSE CASES

Q. Judge Smith, what mistakes do defendants make in civil cases that cause them to lose? Thank you, Roberta

A. Roberta, two frequent unforced errors are ignoring lawsuits for too long and talking to non-lawyers about the specifics of their cases. Let's cover both.

Think of an ostrich—a flightless bird and the largest living bird species. When frightened, an ostrich buries its head in the sand. In its bird brain way of thinking, if it can't see predators, predators can't see it either. The ostrich is, of course, wrong! Instead of being invisible, it becomes a sitting duck (or in this case, a sitting ostrich).

Some defendants mimic ostriches by ignoring lawsuits, deadlines, and the consequences. Their inaction makes them sitting ducks, too. Instead of being killed and eaten, they lose their money, get evicted, or suffer some other bad results they could have prevented by simply responding. Ignoring a legal problem does not make it go away.

The summonses served with lawsuits tell defendants their deadlines for responding. Some defendants hire lawyers to defend them, and others have insurance coverages that provide them with a defense. Some defendants choose to represent themselves, or they opt to do so because they can't afford lawyers.

People with limited funds should seek free or discounted legal services. Those who decide to represent themselves should consider consulting lawyers for advice on how to answer lawsuits, articulate defenses, and prove their defenses at trial. Those who don't risk being penny-wise and dollar-foolish.

People who ignore lawsuits lose their cases by default. Those who do not respond admit the allegations against them and lose their cases by default. Thus, civil defendants should ignore their ostrich impulses and promptly read all the papers served on them, get advice, and take quick and appropriate action. Those with insurance coverage should provide copies of the summonses and lawsuits to their insurance agents and carriers.

The lawyer-client privilege shields private confidential communications between lawyers and clients from disclosure. This privilege encourages clients to divulge everything, so their lawyers can provide them with candid advice and more effective representation.

Blabbermouths talk too much. When civil defendants discuss their cases with non-lawyers, they often make damaging admissions that can be used against them at trial. Roberta, when blabbermouths talk out of turn, they usually pay for it.

There is no substitute for good and timely legal advice from a seasoned lawyer.

CHAPTER 37

TO PLEA OR NOT TO PLEA

Q. Judge Smith, are more cases resolved by plea agreements or trials, and can you explain the plea process? Thank you for helping, Cindy

A. Cindy, dozens of criminal cases are resolved by plea agreements for every criminal case resolved by trial. Now, let's cover the fundamentals of the plea process.

Due process of law requires notice and an opportunity to be heard. In criminal cases, this means defendants are informed about their rights and the charges against them. If they can't afford defense counsel, courts appoint publicly funded lawyers to represent them.

The rules of criminal procedure don't allow trials by ambush, and surprises are frowned upon. Both sides must identify their witnesses, and prosecutors must share incriminating evidence, as well as exonerating evidence, with defendants. Defense lawyers investigate cases, too. Armed with this knowledge and the advice of counsel, defendants can make informed decisions about trying their cases or negotiating plea agreements.

Think of criminal cases as hands of poker. Players must decide whether to play the cards they are dealt or to swap out cards for random draws. Some of the unknown cards in the draw pile are jurors, judges' rulings, and the credibility of witnesses. Some people are better poker players than others, and not everyone has the same tolerance for risk.

Plea agreements are consensual contracts that are negotiated by the parties involved. Only the prosecutor and the defense know how the evidence is stacking up. Only they understand the strengths and weaknesses of their cases, and their unspoken motivations and concerns. Trial judges don't participate in plea negotiations because they don't know these things and must remain neutral.

To use a baseball analogy, judges are like behind-the-plate umpires. Our role is to call balls and strikes and have a consistent strike zone. Judges don't pitch or go to bat for either team, nor do we tell them what their game strategy should be.

When parties strike deals, the specific terms are written up and signed by the prosecutors, defense lawyers, and defendants. Trial judges confirm that defendants understand what they are getting and giving up in return. Typically, courts approve plea agreements when defendants make knowing, intelligent, and voluntary decisions to forgo trials in exchange for the plea terms. Defendants confirm under oath that they understand what they must do to complete their sentences and the potential consequences if they fail to do so.

Open pleas happen when the parties can't agree on plea terms and the defendants choose not to go to trial. Instead, defendants ask judges to impose sentences by exercising their discretion and the defendants agree to accept whatever terms the judges impose. About 96 percent of the county court pleas I approve are plea agreements. The rest are open pleas.

CHAPTER 38

AVOIDING THE SHARK'S HOUSE

My daughter and I recently laughed ourselves silly watching the YouTube posting of a lady explaining why she doesn't swim in the ocean. Her reasoning: "That's the shark's house. If I go there, I'll end up on the shark's plate. If a chicken comes to my house, the chicken will end up on my plate, too."

Restated, the company you keep matters. People and chickens shouldn't go where they can expect trouble, and you shouldn't spend time with abusers, losers, or users. Instead, exercise some common sense and avoid the shark's house.

Q. Judge Smith, you've written about discovery in civil cases. Is there discovery in criminal cases, too? Thanks, George
A. George, Florida courts don't allow trials by ambush. Both sides must identify their witnesses and prosecutors must share incriminating and exonerating evidence with defendants.

The parties don't need the state court's permission to take discovery depositions in felony cases but do need the state court's permission take discovery depositions in misdemeanor cases. In contrast, the federal rules of criminal procedure preclude parties from taking discovery depositions in federal prosecutions.

Q. Judge Smith, voters approved Florida Amendment 4 by more than 64%, and it went into effect on January 8, 2019. How will the law be implemented, and to what extent do you think former felons will be allowed to vote? Thank you, Katrina

A. Katrina, I have served as the chairperson of the Leon County Canvassing Board, which is composed of a county judge, the supervisor of elections, and a county commissioner. Like you, we eagerly await answers to the questions you have posed.

I am sworn to follow the law and will take my direction from the legislature, the appellate courts, and potentially the federal district court. We'll see how it unfolds; the judicial canons I must follow prohibit me from any further comment or speculation.

Q. Judge Smith, you are a county judge, but I've seen you preside over circuit court injunction cases, too. How does that work? — Terri

A. Terri, I am a county judge, but each year I also perform hundreds of hours of circuit court work in my capacity as an "acting circuit judge." Each week, your county judges cover the circuit court's first appearances, search and arrest warrants, and jury qualifications. We also regularly handle injunction dockets and circuit cases assigned to our problem-solving courts. Occasionally, county judges try felony cases and empanel grand juries.

Q. Judge Smith, what happens to people who ignore summonses for jury service? — Wendell
A. Wendell, ignoring a summons for jury service is irresponsible and risky. People with scheduling conflicts should ask the clerk of court to reschedule the dates of their jury service. Those who ignore summonses may have to pay fines, serve time in jail, or both.

CHAPTER 39

NEWTONIAN PHYSICS AND VIOLATIONS OF PROBATION

Q. Judge Smith, what is probation, how it is enforced, and is it fair? Thank you, Phyllis

A. Phyllis, probation is the post-sentence period when the defendant is supervised and he or she must fulfill certain conditions requiring either action, self-control, or restraint. At least 95% of the people on probation chose it by entering into negotiated plea agreements in lieu of jail or prison sentences.

Let's use two examples to explain the concept. First, suppose the state charges a defendant with committing a battery by punching his former girlfriend. Assume he is employed and has no prior criminal record. Rather than sentencing him to jail, he is placed on 12 months of probation. During that time, he must perform 75 hours of community service work, complete an anger management course, and have no direct or indirect contact with the victim. In addition, he must refrain from further criminal activity and pay the victim restitution to cover her medical bills. The goal is to punish the defendant, discourage future violent outbursts, and teach him to control his impulses. Probation protects the victim, too.

Second, suppose the state charges a defendant with driving under the influence of alcohol to the extent that her normal faculties were impaired. Rather than sentencing her to jail, she is placed on 6 months of probation. During that time, she must perform 50 hours of community service, not consume any alcohol, complete a driving-while-impaired deterrence class, complete a victim awareness program; have her vehicle impounded or immobilized for 10 days, and refrain from further criminal activity. By statute, her driver's license will be revoked for a period of 6 months. The goal is to get her alcohol consumption under control, focus her attention on the carnage that impaired drivers cause, and discourage her from driving again while impaired. This protects the rest of us, too.

Defendants are assigned probation officers who supervise their progress and compliance. After defendants fulfill all conditions, their probation is terminated. If they don't fulfill the conditions of their probation, the state may charge them with a violation of probation, which it must prove by the greater weight of the evidence.

According to Isaac Newton's third law of motion, if you push against an object, the object will push back with an equal and opposite force. By analogy, defendants who commit knowing and material violations of probation experience an equal and opposite push back by the courts.

Courts don't expect perfection. Defendants who err but give their best effort and are honest tend to do all right. Courts take into consideration defendants' ability to pay restitution, and unpaid amounts can be reduced to civil judgments. Those who give little to no effort, or lie about it, reap the whirlwind.

Probation is fair. It often provides the structure and incentive some people need to succeed, and most people fulfill their obligations. For those who don't, courts can nullify their prior advantageous sentences and impose harsher sentences instead.

CHAPTER 40

BOXING, WRESTLING, AND CASES IN CONTROVERSY

Q. Judge Smith, what prevents unscrupulous people from staging lawsuits to establish legal precedents? — Riley

A. Riley, few conspirators are smart enough and well-funded enough to perpetrate a fraud on a court. Additionally, most people are bad liars, and even good liars are bad at keeping secrets.

Few conspirators possess the necessary legal knowledge and acting skills to choreograph and present a convincing fake case. Indeed, consider the audience: Trial judges aren't easy to fool.

Furthermore, most conspiracies would require the assistance of a complicit lawyer. Any lawyer caught perpetrating a fraud on the court would face prosecution and disbarment. Likewise, any other conspirator caught perpetrating a fraud on the court would face criminal prosecution and civil sanctions.

Establishing a legal precedent is at least a two-step process. A trial court's final judgment is only binding on the parties, and it takes an appellate decision to establish a binding legal precedent that would apply to other cases. Thus, a conspiracy to establish a specific legal precedent would require enough funding to take the case through a favorably written appellate decision. Most appeals are decided by appellate judges sitting in panels of three or more, and appellate judges are hard to fool, too.

Besides these practical considerations, the law protects us from conspirators by requiring plaintiffs to have "standing" and lawsuits to involve "real cases in controversy."

"Standing" is the capacity of a party to bring a suit in court. To have standing, a plaintiff must have sustained a direct injury or harm that can be remedied. A plaintiff's claim must also be concrete and specific rather than a general grievance. Otherwise, the case will be dismissed for a lack of standing.

The difference between a "real case in controversy" and a "staged case" is like the difference between boxing and professional wrestling. Real cases involve two competitors on opposite sides, both actively competing and trying to win. Staged cases involve two collaborators who actively script and choreograph contrived results. Thus, real cases are like boxing matches, and staged cases are like professional wrestling events (just not as entertaining!)

For those concerned about judges being co-conspirators, no person is above the law. Judges who commit fraud can be removed from office, disbarred, and prosecuted for crimes. The legislature requires judges and executive branch lawyers in leadership positions to make an annual disclosure of their incomes, sources of income, assets, and liabilities. These financial disclosures are designed to reveal potential conflicts of interest, including bribes. Florida's government in the sunshine promotes openness and transparency.

Riley, you can rest assured the litigation that sets legal precedents is the result of active competition and is subject to rigorous checks and balances.

CHAPTER 41

I SAY, YOU SAY, EARL SAY, HEARSAY

Q. Judge Smith, what is "hearsay," why shouldn't juries be allowed to hear it, and is hearsay ever admitted into evidence at trials? — Nate

A. Nate, think of Florida's evidence code as a giant filter. It was designed by the legislature for trial courts to use to screen out evidence that juries shouldn't consider.

At trial, a lawyer presents the evidence he wants the jury to consider, and his opponent must challenge the admissibility of that evidence by voicing timely objections. If a lawyer snoozes, the client loses because any objection not made is waived.

Fact witnesses testify about the relevant facts they know firsthand. Generally, they are asked what they did or didn't do, or what they saw, heard, touched, smelled, or tasted.

In contrast, hearsay is an out-of-court statement offered to prove the truth of the matter asserted. The statement can be oral, written, or nonverbal conduct. Often, hearsay involves an in-court witness repeating what an out-of-court witness said.

Let's use an example. Suppose Juan sues Bobbie for negligence. Juan alleges Bobbie violated his right-of-way and caused a two-car accident. Bobbie denies being at fault, and Juan must prove Bobbie's liability and the amount of damages he suffered.

At trial, Juan's lawyer calls Earl as a witness. Earl testifies he knows nothing about the case except what his friend Sally told him. According to Earl, Sally said that on the day of the accident, she heard Bobbie say, "I ran the dad-gum red light!"

What Sally said, if she said it, is hearsay because it's being offered to prove Bobbie ran the red light and is at fault. If Bobbie's lawyer makes a timely objection, Earl's repetition of what he says Sally said will be excluded from evidence as hearsay.

The law considers hearsay to be less reliable than direct testimony. Why? Let's consider our example. Sally may not even exist. Assuming she does, Sally might be biased, mistaken, or a liar. Bobbie's lawyer can't confront Sally, and the jury can't evaluate her credibility. Moreover, Earl might have lied or misconstrued what Sally said because he was confused, mistaken, or hard of hearing.

Another danger of hearsay is that jurors might substitute the credibility of the in-court witness for the credibility of the out-of-court witness being quoted. After all, Earl might come across as more believable than Sally would. These problems can be avoided by subpoenaing Sally and having her testify at trial.

Now, let's dive into the complexity of applying the rule against hearsay.

If objected to, hearsay evidence is inadmissible unless one of 33 exceptions apply! Moreover, some written and oral statements contain hearsay within hearsay, which adds another layer of analysis.

Hearsay is often admitted into evidence and considered by juries because lawyers don't object, or one of the 33 exceptions applies.

Let's close with just two examples of commonly applied hearsay exceptions.

The business records exception applies to records regularly kept in the ordinary course of business. Record keepers must have firsthand knowledge of the events or transactions they record, and the record must be made at or near the time it happened.

The excited utterance exception applies to the out-of-court statements made in reaction to startling events or conditions. Excited utterances are blurted out under the stress of the moment and happen so quickly that the declarant didn't have time to reflect or fabricate.

CHAPTER 42

THE ABCS OF ATTORNEY FEES

This is the first of two chapters about attorney fees. This chapter will cover who is responsible for paying attorney fees. Next chapter, I'll explain how "reasonable attorney fees" are determined.

Q. Judge Smith, under what circumstances can one party be forced to pay the opposing party's attorney fees? Thank you, Jessie

A. Jessie, generally each party is responsible for paying his or her own attorneys, but three notable exceptions may apply:

1) A statute may require the losing party to pay the winning party's attorney fees;

2) A contract may require the losing party to pay the winning party's attorney fees; and

3) The court may order one party to pay another's attorney fee as a sanction for misbehavior.

Let's discuss some examples.

By Law

The Legislature has enacted statutes that require one party to pay another party's attorney fees. Often, this is done to encourage reasonable settlements, discourage frivolous lawsuits, or to level the playing field. For example, most residential landlord-tenant eviction cases involve questions about the payment of rent. Usually, the tenant either paid the rent on time or he didn't; the law requires the loser of the case to pay the winner's attorney fees.

Another example is one involving insurance claims. If, for example, a contractor's general liability insurance company denies coverage of a claim, the contractor could defend the claim and sue the insurance company to enforce his contractual rights.

If the insurance company is found to have wrongfully denied the claim, it must reimburse the contractor for the attorney fees he incurred defending himself and enforcing his contractual rights. If the insurance company rightfully denied the claim, the contractor doesn't have to reimburse his insurer for the attorney fees it incurred.

By Contract

Parties to a written contract usually negotiate terms, which often include a clause for attorney fees. Based on the terms of the contract, if a lawsuit is filed, the loser must reimburse the winner's reasonable attorney fees. Examples of contracts that frequently include attorney fees clauses are installment loan contracts, commercial landlord-tenant leases, and non-compete agreements.

As Sanctions for Bad Behavior

Sometimes parties ignore or stonewall discovery deadlines or engage in other poor conduct that causes unnecessary work, delays, and expenses. If their misbehavior is egregious enough, courts can require them to reimburse opposing parties' related attorney fees to discourage future bad behavior.

Suppose defense counsel must file a motion and attend a hearing to compel the plaintiff to turn over requested documents. As a sanction, the court might order the plaintiff to pay defense counsel for two hours of her time.

CHAPTER 43

PROFESSOR PLUM GETS A CLUE

Background: Civil trial lawyers sell their time, experience, and track records for delivering results. Based on supply and demand, they charge what the market will support. Most civil trial lawyers bill their time at agreed hourly rates or charge contingency fees based on the results obtained.

Q. Judge Smith, how do courts decide the amount of attorney fees the winning party should be awarded? — Vickie

A. Vickie, trial courts hold evidentiary hearings and follow the criteria and guidance established by the appellate courts.

Suppose Professor Plum loans Miss Scarlet money, and the two enter into a contract that allows the prevailing party to recover his or her attorney fees. When Miss Scarlet defaults by failing to make her monthly payments, Professor Plum sues her for breach of contract. He wins at trial, and a local jury awards him damages.

Afterward, a hearing is scheduled to determine how much Miss Scarlet owes Professor Plum to cover his attorney fees. Determining this amount will hinge on three factors.

How Much Lawyer Time Was Needed?

The first factor is, how much lawyer time was needed, considering the novelty and difficulty of the case? Professor Plum's lawyer will provide the court with her billing records and give a thorough explanation of what she did and why. Her time will be scrutinized, and she will be subject to cross-examination.

Lawyers must justify the time they bill, and courts must determine whether their legal work was necessary and performed efficiently. Courts cut unnecessary, duplicative, and wasteful time. Let's suppose Professor Plum's lawyer billed him for 76 hours, the court approved 72.8 hours and disallowed 3.2 hours.

What is a Reasonable Hourly Rate?

The second factor is, what is a reasonable hourly rate for the legal services rendered? According to case law, a reasonable hourly rate "is the prevailing market rate in the relevant legal community for similar lawyers of reasonably comparable skills, experience, and reputation." Suppose Professor Plum paid his lawyer $300 an hour, but the going rate for equivalent lawyers is $250 an hour. The court will approve $250 as the reasonable hourly rate. Professor Plum can pay his lawyer an extra $50 an hour, but Miss Scarlet only must pay the going rate.

Should a Multiplier be Applied?

The third factor is whether the court applies a multiplier. It's hard to convince lawyers to take on high-risk, work-intensive cases unless there is the potential for a good payday.

When appropriate, courts apply multipliers to adjust attorney fees to reward lawyers for taking on difficult cases. Encouraging lawyers to litigate difficult cases for enhanced attorney fees provides access to courts for regular people who couldn't otherwise afford counsel.

What He Asked For, What He Got, and What Might Have Been

In our example, Professor Plum sought to recover attorney fees totaling $22,800 ($300 x 76 = $22,800), without the application of a multiplier. Instead, the court awarded him $18,200 ($250 x 72.8 = $18,200).

Suppose Professor Plum's claim for attorney fees had justified the use of a 1.5x multiplier. If so, the court would have awarded him $27,300 ($250 x 72.8 x 1.5 = $27,300). Collection is a horse of a different color.

CHAPTER 44
INQUESTS OF THE DEAD

As your county judge, I routinely handle warrants, first appearances, hearings, and trials involving illegal drugs. Let's cover five common fact patterns that focus on how drugs destroy lives in our community.

A Skeleton Named Bob

A picture really is worth a thousand words. In 2014, when he was arrested for possession of marijuana, Bob was 6'3," 215 pounds, chiseled, and healthy. Four years later, Bob died of an overdose of methamphetamine. By then, his skin was covered with pockmarked sores, and his weight had dropped to 119 pounds. He died the day before his 24th birthday, a skeleton named Bob.

What Happened to Hanna

Hanna was popular, a varsity athlete, and on the homecoming

court. She was also insecure, succumbed to peer pressure, and started taking drugs. Things quickly spun out of control. Within weeks of dropping out of school, a predator "befriended" her and soon she became a victim of human trafficking. Her drug supplier controlled her, beat her, sold her body, and kept all the money. When she got pregnant, he paid for the abortion. Hanna caught a venereal disease, and she's been arrested for solicitation.

The Wisdom of Three Dog Night

Do you remember the band "Three Dog Night" and its song "Momma Told Me?" Murder and mayhem break out when drug deals go bad. As it turns out, the same people who want illegal drugs also want easy money, and drug deals offer access to both. Think of it as one-stop shopping. So, Momma was right, and participating in a drug deal "ain't the way to have fun, son!"

Poisoned, Allergic Reaction, or Overdose

Drug traffickers cut their products to stretch quantities and maximize profits by adulterating the purity of the base drug. Adding too much of an ingredient, the wrong ingredient, or the wrong combination of ingredients renders a drug deadly. Even benign mixes can trigger deadly allergic reactions. Because the mix will always be unknown, shooting up with street heroin is no different than playing Russian roulette with a loaded gun.

For years, Johnny was a functioning heroin addict. Today, after shooting up, he died. What caused his death? Was his heroin poisonous? Did he suffer a fatal allergic reaction to an ingredient? Or did he simply take too much and die from an overdose?

By statute, under the right circumstances, a county judge can conduct an "inquest of the dead" hearing to determine the cause of death.

Jake's Shake Goes Up in Smoke

In fairness to Jake, who has regularly smoked marijuana for more than 25 years, pot has not been a gateway drug. He has never progressed to harder drugs. Instead, marijuana has sapped his soul and killed his ambitions. As a result, he's 40, single, unemployed, and living in his brother's garage.

Don't be like Bob, Hanna, Johnny, or Jake. If you need help, reach out before it's too late. Your community cares about you and we need you.

CHAPTER 45

SIGNS AND INTERVENTIONS

If asked, while in the grip of a substance abuse disorder, most people won't fess up about their addictions. Instead, they're more likely to deny or minimize the full extent of their dependency. Over time, these denials and minimizations can alienate family, friends and employers.

How strong are addictions? Strong enough that when confronted with the choice, people with untreated substance use disorders might surrender love, security, success, reputation, and/or health to their addictions. Now, let's discuss common signs of addiction and what to do in response.

Signs of Addiction (Non-Exhaustive List)

Family, friends, and employers should be on the lookout for physical symptoms and changes in behavior.

Physical symptoms often include: bloodshot or glazed eyes; dilated or constricted pupils; abrupt weight changes; track marks; and/or sleep disturbance (too much or too little).

Behavioral changes often include: increased aggression or irritability; unexpected and rapid changes in attitude/personality; increased depression; changes in friends and social groups; dramatic changes in habits/priorities; withdrawal; changes in wardrobe to cover needle marks; lying to conceal routines; and criminal acts (to fund the habit).

How to Respond

Pray for them! Let them know that you care and are concerned. Rally their other family and friends to do likewise. Observe, talk, ask questions, and listen. Arrange for the people who matter most to them to intervene. Take them to their primary health care providers (or other health care providers) for evaluation and ask their doctors for referrals to substance abuse providers.

Treatment can include: detoxification (usually 2-3 days); long-term inpatient care; and/or outpatient care. Determine if health insurance is available to cover costs.

Threats and demands typically don't work. Instead, figure out what will motivate someone with a substance use disorder to seek professional help and follow through. If confronted with dire circumstances, petition the circuit court to compel the addict to undergo evaluation and short-term treatment (Florida's Marchman Act).

If a loved one or friend is prosecuted for an addiction-related crime, explore having his or her case transferred to Leon County's Drug and Alcohol Rehabilitation Court.

CHAPTER 46

NOTICE AND AN OPPORTUNITY TO BE HEARD

The British Navy deprived Americans of their liberty by kidnapping them, placing them on British ships, and forcing them to serve the Crown or walk the plank. The British Army deprived Americans of their property by occupying their homes and eating their food without permission or compensation. These abuses served as catalysts for the Third Amendment, regarding the quartering of soldiers, and the Fifth Amendment, regarding of due process of law.

Q. Judge Smith, what is due process of law? Jules
A. Jules, a fundamental difference between the United States and other nations is our adherence to the rule of law and due process of law. It's not exaggerating to suggest we owe our many freedoms and national development to these twin pillars

of the law.

The rule of law is a simple concept. The laws enacted by Congress and the state legislature apply to everyone, and no one is above or below the law. Now, let's focus on due process of law.

The original 13 colonies were founded by people who immigrated here in search of opportunity and religious freedom, and to escape over-reaching by the government. Agriculture dominated the economies of the colonies, so consider how much nerve, blind faith, and work ethic it took to establish homes, plant and harvest crops, and survive in the wilderness with no safety net.

Given these immense challenges, the people expected the government to protect their property interests rather than confiscating them. Likewise, the people expected to live free from undue government interference with their lives and liberty. Our guarantee that the government fulfills these expectations is due process of law.

Due process of law is so important that it's the only substantive phrase repeated in the U.S. Constitution. The Fifth and Fourteenth Amendments, respectively, prohibit the federal government and state governments from depriving any person of "life, liberty, or property, without due process of law." In this context, life involves death penalty cases, liberty involves involuntary confinements, and property involves uncompensated takings.

Before the government can take people's lives, liberty or property, they must be put on notice and provided with an opportunity to be heard. Diligent-good-faith efforts must be made to find people and service of notice on them should be hand delivered when practical. The opportunity to be heard includes the right to counsel and a fair and impartial process. The goal is to reach just decisions on the merits.

Think of due process as a floor and not a ceiling. It provides the minimum level of protection that must be afforded. Although, perhaps we could do more, we can do no less. Every day, in courtrooms throughout America, judges safeguard the people's right to due process of law. I invite you to visit a courthouse and see for yourself.

PART V

BEING A LAWYER

CHAPTER 47

THE BENEFIT OF EXPERIENCE

Q. Judge Smith, I am finishing up my last semester of high school and have applied for admission to several colleges. After college, I want to study law. How important will my choice of college be to law school admission committees? Also, what should I do in college to prepare for law school? Thank you, Katie

A. Katie, I am excited for you! Most law school admission committees will be more influenced by how you perform in college than they'll be by where you went to college. My advice is to pick a school where you will thrive and can obtain a good and affordable education.

Evaluate your college options by comparing schools' academic reputations and then contrasting their annual costs for tuition and room-and-board. Also consider the distance between your home and each campus, and factor in round trip travel costs and travel time. I suggest researching and applying for school specific scholarships and grants.

If your budget is tight, consider attending a community college for two years, and then completing your bachelor's degree at a state university. By working part-time jobs, you can cover some of the costs of your education while strengthening your resume. Student loans are an option, but don't run up too much debt or waste borrowed money.

Now, let's consider your major. Law schools don't prefer one major over another. What matters most is that you push yourself. Take courses that interest you and will require you to read, write, think, and excel at communicating by the spoken and written word.

Don't ignore your common sense and remember the lessons and moral grounding that your family taught you. Be open-minded, and soak up all the knowledge you can, but don't believe everything you hear or read. Great lawyers are confirmed skeptics who live by the phrases "show me," "prove it," and "justify yourself."

Extracurricular activities provide you an opportunity to distinguish yourself from other prospective law students. Seek out extracurricular activities that you will enjoy and become actively involved. Assume a leadership position or two and be a difference maker.

Grades matter a lot. Your admission to a law school of choice will be based largely on your college grade point average and your law school entrance exam (LSAT) score. Give both your concentrated best effort.

Good character matters because the state bar will investigate your application for membership. If you're deemed unfit, you'll be denied a license to practice law. Accordingly, don't give anyone any reason to question your honesty, reliability, or sobriety. At a minimum, obey the law and avoid becoming an alcoholic, drug addict, or gambling addict.

Have fun, too, and enjoy the journey. Good luck, Katie!

CHAPTER 48

BECOMING LAWYERS

Q. Judge Smith, how do people become lawyers? Thank you, Freda

A. Freda, some say that lawyers, being reptiles, are hatched. Others say, based on the sheer numbers of them, lawyers are produced at manufacturing plants.

All kidding aside, becoming a lawyer is like running a gauntlet—more marathon than sprint. The pathway to bar membership is a filter that protects the public by screening the people who become licensed attorneys. It is designed to weed out those who'll lack the necessary competence, moral character, and fitness.

Aspiring lawyers must earn bachelor's degrees, achieve high scores on the Law School Admissions Test, and successfully compete with other applicants to gain admission to law schools. Law school admission committees focus heavily on academics, test scores, and character. Having well-rounded and diverse classes is an important consideration, too. It takes three academic years to earn a law degree.

Each state licenses and regulates the members of its bar. Before a lawyer can be licensed, he or she must demonstrate a functional understanding of the state's law and its rules of procedure.

Because character always matters, state bars conduct extensive character investigations to screen applicants for fitness issues. Fitness includes good morals, self-control, lawfulness, financial responsibility, and mental health stability.

Evaluating someone's fitness to practice law requires a careful balance between extending grace to people who've made mistakes and adequately protecting the public. This includes considering and addressing applicants' mental health and substance abuse issues.

Being a lawyer is a position of trust that requires competence, honesty, and reliability. Bar applicants deemed by a state's bar to lack the good moral character and fitness to practice law will be denied membership in that state's bar.

The bar applicants who are deemed morally sound and fit must pass the state's bar examination, a multi-state bar examination, and a legal ethics test. Not everybody can meet these strict requirements. The legal profession protects the public by screening law students and applicants for bar membership.

CHAPTER 49

LETTER TO A LAW SCHOOL GRADUATE

Congratulations—graduating from law school is a milestone! Take time to celebrate your achievement with family and friends, and tomorrow you can refocus on passing the bar exam and finding a job.

Good fortune has already smiled on you. Your chosen profession will open doors for you in private practice, public service, business, and government. With continued effort and focus, you can earn a good living and be a difference maker.

Only you can decide how to live and what you want to accomplish in your career. So, think big and aim high. Stay humble and pay your dues, because you still have a lot to learn, and there is no substitute for actual experience. Be patient. The key to success is earning the confidence of others through sustained effort and high achievement over an extended period.

Diligently protect your reputation by being honest and avoiding appearances of impropriety. Having good character and a reputation for fairness will serve you well.

You can avoid scandal, prison, heartache, and disbarment by following this simple advice: Don't do or say anything that you wouldn't do or say in front of your mother or the sheriff.

People notice how you treat others, including the janitor, your paralegal, and opposing counsel. Show respect to everyone and be plain-spoken. Make it a habit to introduce yourself and network with a purpose.

Do you want to be a successful trial lawyer? Visit your local courthouse and observe how skilled lawyers and judges handle hearings and trials. Screen out and eliminate bad cases up front. Outwork your opponents, but don't overreach, and remember to adopt a style suitable to your personality.

Great trial lawyers are great storytellers! Tell simple, direct, and memorable stories. Remember that juries are more likely to return favorable verdicts if your presentation at trial involves a combination of visual, auditory, and kinetic learning.

Try to listen twice as much as you speak, because when you are new, you don't have a clue. Your doctorate-level vocabulary is a gift and a curse, so craft your words to strike a chord with your target audience.

A good trial lawyer is a born skeptic who prepares, questions, clarifies, and communicates. Be well-read and stay current with popular culture. You never know when information, a well-turned phrase, or a cultural reference will come in handy. Finally, be a community leader and stretch beyond your comfort zone. Good luck, and I hope to see you in my courtroom.

CHAPTER 50

MURDER, CANNIBALISM, AND GOVERNMENT CONSPIRACY

Q. Judge Smith, my daughter tells me about the interesting cases she reads in law school. We want to know if you had a favorite law school class, and if any of the cases you read as a student still stand out? — Lisa

A. Lisa, criminal law was my favorite class, and a British case involving murder, cannibalism, and government conspiracy immediately comes to mind! Here's what happened in the infamous case of *Regina v. Dudley and Stephens*, 14 Q.B.D 273 (1884).

A storm forced three sailors and a cabin boy to abandon ship and take refuge in a tiny lifeboat 1,600 miles from land. They had no drinking water, except for rain, and no food except for two one-pound tins of turnips and a turtle. They suffered from constant thirst, hunger, and exposure to the elements.

By the 20th day, the cabin boy was weak, listless, and clinging to life. The three sailors discussed sacrificing him, so that they might live. One refused, but the other two (Dudley and Stephens) slit the cabin boy's throat. Afterward, all three men fed on his body and blood. Days later, the three sailors were rescued by a passing ship, "alive but in the lowest state of prostration."

News reports of the survivors' ordeal, including the lurid details, fascinated and horrified British society. Although not the first incident of cannibalism on the high seas, this instance was the most publicized. Other sailors facing group dehydration and starvation had cast lots, killed the losers, and cannibalized the corpses.

Simply put, Queen Victoria and the elites of Britain were appalled. In response, they conspired to prevent "killing for cannibalism" from becoming an accepted maritime practice. Thus, Dudley and Stephens were prosecuted for murder to establish a legal precedent.

Fearing a jury would acquit them due to extreme circumstances, British officials choreographed the desired outcome. Instead of following the normal protocol and asking the jury to decide the defendants' guilt or innocence, the trial judge instructed the jury to answer two questions:

1) Assuming the cabin boy had not been killed, would he have died anyhow from natural causes?

2) Assuming the three men had not fed on the dead

boy's body and blood, would they have died before being rescued?

The evidence presented at trial was stacked to ensure the jury would answer yes to both questions, and it did.

Afterward, an appellate court was asked if the defendants' need for survival excused the killing, or if the killing was murder nonetheless. The defense argued the sacrifice of a doomed boy was justified because it saved three lives. The appellate court disagreed, and as planned, ruled that "necessity or duress" doesn't excuse the taking of a human life.

As a result, Dudley and Stephens were convicted of murder and sentenced to death. Having established the desired legal precedent, Queen Victoria commuted the defendants' sentences to time served and both were set free. Lisa, thank you for this trip down memory lane.

CHAPTER 51

THE LAWYERS KNOW TOO MUCH

A stanza from a Carl Sandburg poem reads:

"Why is there always a secret singing, when a lawyer cashes in? / Why does a hearse horse snicker, hauling a lawyer away?"

Sandburg provides his answer to these questions in the poem's title, "The Lawyers Know Too Much."

Q. Judge Smith, what is the meaning of the legal term *discovery*, and can you provide examples to explain the concept?
Thank you, Laura

A. Laura, discovery involves gathering and exchanging case-related information, and providing sworn answers to case-related questions. This is accomplished by interrogatories, requests for admission, requests to produce, and depositions. Let's discuss each discovery tool, and I'll provide examples.
Interrogatories are written questions from one party to another. They must be answered truthfully in writing, subject to the penalties of perjury.

Suppose the plaintiff in a car accident case sues the owner of the other vehicle to recover damages. Because she claims lost income, the defendant needs to determine her work history and compensation before and after the accident. To gather this information, the defendant might serve the plaintiff with interrogatories asking about her education, training, dates of employment, and rates of pay.

It's wasteful to litigate undisputed facts, and requests for admission allow parties to ask their opponents to admit uncontested facts that are relevant to the case. In our example, the plaintiff might ask the defendant to admit "at the time of the collision, the truck driven by the defendant rear-ended the car driven by the plaintiff."

Often, parties need access to documents or tangible things possessed or controlled by others. They can gain access to information by serving their opponents with requests to produce, or by subpoenaing information from third parties. In the car accident case, the defendant might request the plaintiff produce her W-2 statements to confirm her income, and her medical records to verify her injuries and the status of her health.

Parties frequently use a combination of interrogatories, requests for admission, and requests to produce to gather the information they need to take depositions. Discovery depositions are sworn oral testimonies that are recorded and can be transcribed.

During depositions, lawyers should ask questions directly related to the case or "reasonably calculated to lead to the discovery of admissible evidence." Lawyers ask open-ended questions to gather information and narrow questions to lock in answers. At trial, they make use of deposition testimony to ask adverse witnesses leading questions and to impeach witnesses who change their stories.

Discovery reveals the strengths and weaknesses of cases, prevents surprises, and promotes settlements or decisions on the merits. Good lawyers use discovery to learn enough about their cases. Bad lawyers abuse discovery by overdoing it and being inefficient and repetitious. Thus, the secret singings and hearse horses' snickers should be reserved for them, because bad lawyers often do know too much.

PART VI

GOING FORWARD

CHAPTER 52

DAD WAS SPECIAL AND PLAN WHILE YOU CAN

In 1934, my paternal grandfather, an avowed Roosevelt Democrat, asked my grandmother to name their unborn son "Franklin Delano Smith." It had somehow escaped him that she was a Republican. So instead, when my Grandmother signed my dad's birth certificate, she named him "Franklin Demar Smith."

Dad always joked he was lucky he wasn't named "Herbert Hoover Smith," but he was lucky for many other reasons. He and my mom, Janice, were happily married for more than 66 years, and they raised two children, four grandchildren, and two great-grandchildren.

When Dad graduated from high school, he wanted to go to college but couldn't afford it. Newly married, he took the first job he was offered. As fate would have it, that job was in construction, installing industrial insulation. Between 1952 and 1961, he was exposed to insulation products containing asbestos.

Back then, no one told him, or the men he worked with, that asbestos is a lethal carcinogen. When inhaled, an asbestos fiber can lay dormant in a human body for decades before manifesting as terminal cancer. Over the years, Dad lost countless friends to asbestos-related cancers.

In the early 1960s, he transitioned from field work to management, and beginning in 1973, became a successful insulation contractor. Frank took care of his employees, and they loved and respected him for it.

My dad, age 85, died of mesothelioma on November 15, 2019. It's not a quick or easy way to die, but true to form, he was brave and dignified through the end. We comforted him, and his faith in Jesus Christ reassured him. My father taught me life lessons and you can follow his example, too. How, you ask?

Put family first and plan while you can. Nobody lives forever, so prepare for your death before it's too late. Your failure to plan will burden your family, compound their grief, and waste time and money.

Get legal advice and execute a will. Otherwise, the legislature decides how your property will be distributed. Plan your estate to avoid probate whenever possible, and organize your assets, liabilities, and insurance policies so your survivors aren't left guessing.

Execute a living will, and pre-plan your funeral and burial

arrangements. Don't forget to arrange loving homes for the pets you'll leave behind. Share this information with others and tell your loved ones that you love them. Reconcile with people and make peace with God.

Franklin Demar Smith was generous, and he made sure that his children and grandchildren earned college and post-graduate degrees without having any debt. He took good care of Mom and our family and enjoyed life to the fullest. Not a bad legacy for a pipe-coverer from Alabama.

CHAPTER 53

RHETT BUTLER AND E PLURIBUS UNUM

Q. Judge Smith, we seem more divided and ruder than ever, and it's hard to discuss civics without civility. What do you think, and how do we make it better? — Ruth

A. Well, Ruth, as your county judge, I am responsible for maintaining proper courtroom decorum. People know to be on time, polite, and respectful. That includes the attorneys!

Outside of my courtroom is a different story. There, good manners, clean language, and civility are in short supply. My dad always taught me that people who resort to swearing suffer from poor vocabularies. Consider that 80 years ago, Hollywood censors had to approve Rhett Butler's use of the word *damn* in the movie "Gone with the Wind."

The First Amendment promotes free speech and the "marketplace of ideas." The government doesn't censor or suppress speech. Rather, it's as American as apple pie for the people to express all sides of an issue—and may the best ideas win!

Dictators and tyrants don't like the marketplace of ideas (think Hitler, Castro, and Mao Zedong). Fortunately for us, democracy does!

Kids learn manners and civility by observing adults. So, let's set good examples for them.

Now, Ruth, you asked if we are more divided than ever. My answer is no. Our unity waxes and wanes over time.

The original 13 colonies were formed and governed separately. People immigrated here seeking religious freedom, land, and new opportunities. Those who survived were tough and self-reliant. They had no infrastructure or welfare state to fall back on. The settlers, pioneers, and trailblazers from our history continue to influence us. We unite when facing a common threat or foe (think World War II and 9/11), and we divide when competing among ourselves.

Our oldest national motto is "E pluribus unum," which is Latin for "from many—one." This motto fits because the 13 colonies became states and then united together to form "a more perfect union." "E pluribus unum" is proudly displayed on our coins and the $1 bill.

Imagine our nation's history as a giant pendulum that swings to and fro. Suppose that the "pendulum bob," the round disk at the bottom of the pendulum, is symbolic for "E pluribus unum". At one extreme, we are fully united. At the opposite extreme, we are fully divided. Over time, depending on the direction and speed of the pendulum, we are somewhere in between. That's who we are.

CHAPTER 54

TIME TRAVEL AND KEEPING IT REAL

Because we enjoy the freedoms of speech and press, we can question and criticize our governments and political leaders without fear of governmental reprisals. This encourages robust debates and the vetting of issues. Vigorous competition in the "marketplace of ideas" fosters good public policy and accountability.

Although the First and Fourteenth Amendments protect us from abuses by our governments, they don't protect us from each other. Today, people are less inclined to listen to one another, communicate in good faith, and give one another the benefit of the doubt. With civility and empathy in short supply, now is the time to focus on our blessings and adjust our perspectives.

No matter what social issues confront us, we are lucky to live in the here and now. Indeed, if time travel was possible, I suspect few of us would choose to live in any other time or place. Consider life without electricity, air conditioning, or modern medicine, and just imagine dentistry without Novocain. Yikes!

When the American colonies declared their independence from Great Britain, Thomas Jefferson wrote that "all men are created equal." Ever since, our quest for equality for everyone has both inspired and challenged us. Fortunately, our Founders established limited governments that are stable but flexible enough to adapt.

Like us, our Founders and forbearers were all too human and far from perfect. Like us, they were not saints, nor did they need to be. They have earned our adulation but are not above reproach for their shortcomings.

The danger we face judging previous generations by today's standards is that future generations will judge us by their standards, too. If this happens, we will fare no better than those who came before us.

Over time, we fought and won a bloody civil war, abolished slavery, and expanded suffrage. We amended the law to promote equal protection and civil rights. No other nation in world history compares as favorably, and few would prefer citizenship elsewhere.

We are multifaceted and can cherish our common heritage as Americans while simultaneously identifying with the things that make us different and distinct. It doesn't have to be one or the other. Rather, it can and should be both.

Let's renew our efforts to be polite, kind, and respectful to one another. Let's do a better job of listening, communicating, and working through the issues that threaten to divide us. After all, as friends and countrymen, we should be willing to walk an occasional mile in the other fellow's shoes.

ACKNOWLEDGEMENTS

Taking the long view, many people contributed to the writing of this book, including my parents, Frank and Janice Smith, and my two favorite school teachers, Maye Walker and Norma Hodges. It was my father who first suggested I attend law school.

I owe my legal education to The Florida State University College of Law, Talbot "Sandy" D'Alemberte, Charles Ehrhardt, Nat Stern, and Paul Jess.

My 24 years working as a private practice trial lawyer were invaluable, as were my four years working in Florida's executive branch of government. I owe my public service opportunities to Jason Gonzalez, Jeff Woodburn, Ben Gibson, Rick Figlio, Ken Lawson, and my local judicial nominating committee. They literally opened doors for me, as did Florida Governor Rick Scott, who appointed me to the county bench. Most of all, I am humbled by and grateful to the voters of Leon County, Florida, who elected me to be their county judge.

This book wouldn't exist without two patient and dynamic women. I am indebted to my friend Sandi Poreda for her advice and editing skills. I also owe a special thanks to my dear wife Cindy, who has indulged me and edited each chapter an infinite number of times.

Writers need deadlines and outlets and my local newspaper provided both. This book wouldn't exist without the *Tallahassee Democrat*, Martha Gruender, and the Gannett family of newspapers. They syndicated my "Ask Judge Smith" column.

Likewise, I appreciate Real Talk Radio 93.3 FM in Tallahassee, Florida, co-host Greg Tish, and co-host/producer Rob MacDonald-Davies for airing the "Ask Judge Smith" radio program.

Thank you each for your contribution, encouragement, and occasional push.

J. Layne Smith
Leon County Judge
Florida's Second Judicial Circuit

ABOUT THE AUTHOR

The Honorable J. Layne Smith is a county judge in Leon County, Florida. A legal scholar, Smith graduated in the top 6 percent of his law school class. He was previously a successful private practice civil, criminal, and administrative trial lawyer for twenty-four years. He then served four years in state government as the general counsel to two Florida state agencies and as a state retirement commissioner. For decades, he has held Martindale-Hubbell's highest ratings for legal skills and ethics.

Smith lives in Tallahassee, Florida, with his wife, Cindy. In his spare time, he can be found reading, writing, and spending time with family, friends, and his dog Barley. He is a passionate fan of college sports, particularly football. Go Seminoles and Roll Tide!

Made in the USA
Coppell, TX
25 June 2026

83143315R00134